£450

Ulster at the Crossroads

ULSTER AT THE CROSSROADS

by

TERENCE O'NEILL

with an introduction by

John Cole

FABER AND FABER

London

First published in 1969
by Faber and Faber Limited
24 Russell Square London WC1
Printed in Great Britain by
Latimer Trend & Co Ltd Plymouth
All rights reserved

SBN 571 09253 5

Contents

Introduction

Northern Ireland at its birth was an unwanted baby. Its
people had no desire for their state to be created. I believe
their instincts to have been sound. Economically and socially,
Ulster could have developed further and faster, it could have
led a calmer and more civilized existence, as a part of the
United Kingdom which had no separate legislature. But that
was not the issue in the stormy years between 1910 and 1921.
The six north-eastern counties which were to form Northern
Ireland were engulfed in the wider tragedy of Ireland. Indeed,
it was a broader drama still, for the struggle of Ireland to be
independent was the first scene in a gradual and continuous
crumbling of the British Empire, perhaps of the concept of
empire as a system of government.

From the start the Ulster state has been a deeply divided
community. For while a majority of its people, the Protestants, would have been happy to continue under direct rule
from Westminster, the one-third of the population that was
Catholic wanted to be part of the Irish Free State. The creation of the Ulster Parliament and Government was an attempt
to reconcile the irreconcilable, to bundle both sets of aspirations into a shabby compromise: the Protestants could accept
it as maintaining their position within the Union; the Catholics
could hope that the Parliaments in Dublin and Belfast would
eventually create the projected Council of Ireland (a body
which never progressed beyond the pages of the 1920 Government of Ireland Act).

INTRODUCTION

The tragedy of Ulster is the conservatism which has kept that basic quarrel unresolved through nearly fifty years of turbulent history. The Catholic minority have held aloof from the state, both in sentiment and in practice; the Protestant majority have not in their hearts accepted Catholics as equal partners. The raw edges of antagonism have worn down over the years, but the underlying loyalties have not changed. It is idle to argue who is to blame, whether the chicken or the egg came first. The quarrel nowadays has a certain air of ludicrous anachronism. Do the sub-editors on Irish Nationalist papers, I wonder, still struggle to get 'Six Counties Prime Minister' into a narrow headline to avoid the forbidden use of 'Ulster' or 'N.I.'? Do obituaries in Unionist papers still describe the Unionist as 'staunch', but the Nationalist as 'convinced', thus carrying the value judgements of their politics beyond the grave?

I would think not. Indeed, I know that this essay, written by an Ulsterman who has lived in England for thirteen years, will draw the charge that times have changed beyond recognition, that my analysis is out of touch and out of date (though the events of 1969 which forced the resignation of Terence O'Neill may have made critics less sure of themselves). During a political recollection that goes back for more than a quarter of a century, I have rarely been without acquaintances in Ulster who detected a millennium that was just around the corner. Yet in the nature of things revolutionary change is improbable. Attitudes certainly have changed, though not so much, in the eye of the occasional visitor, as people in Ulster imagine. What remains unchanged and perhaps unchangeable is the situation: and Ulster's is a situation tragi-comedy, with both sides caught in postures that are not wholly of their own choosing.

Men like Terence O'Neill would be justly angry if you suggested that they believed in single-party government. The crude propagandists of Irish unity have long exploited public abhorrence of Nazism and Communism by blaming the Unionists for staying in uninterrupted power for forty-eight years. The real culprit is the abiding dispute about Northern Ireland's right to exist. This has made the permanence of Unionist rule inevitable, though no less corrosive of healthy democratic politics for that. All the charge and counter-charge about gerrymandering and discrimination ought not to obscure the fact that throughout the past century the overwhelming majority of electors have wanted the Union with Britain to continue. What O'Neill tried to do, within an intractable frame of reference, was so to draw the sting of ancient sectarian bitternesses as to create a new situation. If he had succeeded, it would have meant that normal twentieth-century politics, based on a division between Right and Left, might one day exist.

It is difficult to know at what date an historical background should begin. In a country of long memories, most writers' preference would be for the Plantation, the period in the seventeenth century when Scots and English settled in the North of Ireland. But the politico-religious division does not stretch without interruption from then until now.

By the end of the eighteenth century the Northern Presbyterians were Ireland's leading radicals, men under the influence of the American and French revolutions. They joined with Catholics in the Society of United Irishmen and in the rising of 1798. These efforts to unite Protestant and Catholic died in the nineteenth century, first as the Presbyterians achieved civil rights for themselves, then as Catholic Emancipation began to make all the Protestants uncomfortably aware that Ireland had a Catholic majority.

Gladstone's conversion to Home Rule raised for the Ulster Protestants, and particularly for the Orangemen, the spectre of 'Rome Rule' from Dublin. Perhaps from that moment the laager mentality, from which many of them suffer even today, became inevitable. When Asquith's Government returned to Home Rule in 1910, at least two members of the Cabinet, Lloyd George and Churchill, understood enough of the complications of Irish politics to wish to have the North excluded from the Bill and from the proposed Irish Free State. Eleven years and a World War later this was the solution that was reached, but in the meantime Protestant and Catholic opinion had polarised. In two generations the scars of the years 1910–21 have scarcely faded. The Protestants' trauma was the bitter paradox that they, who were more royalist than the King, should be threatened with expulsion from the kingdom by his forces. For the Catholics it was the fear that they were to be excluded from the independent Ireland they had cherished for so long.

The Protestants' self-reliance and assertiveness were hardened in the years before the Great War, when by signing the Ulster Covenant they pledged themselves to resist Home Rule, and by creating the Ulster Volunteer Force and running guns from Germany and elsewhere they prepared themselves to carry out the threat. Ironically and tragically, the Covenant was sealed with bloodshed not against British or rival Irish armies, but when the U.V.F., four years later, was cut to pieces by German machine-guns on the Somme.

Though many Catholics fought in the war, their folk-heroes were not those of the Somme, but the men who gave their lives for Irish liberty in the Easter Rising of 1916. Fifty years later, both sacrifices are still being celebrated, and they have added a new dimension to the division in Ulster life.

By the summer of 1914, the British Cabinet had decided that Partition was the only solution. Churchill has immortalised —in condescending words that became all too typical of English ennui about Ireland—the hardening divisions of opinion. In

1914, he wrote, the Cabinet had 'toiled round the muddy by-ways of Fermanagh and Tyrone', but without success. The declaration of war interrupted their efforts.

By 1918, 'every institution, almost in the world is strained, great empires have been overturned. The whole map of Europe has been changed. The position of countries has been violently altered. The mode and thought of men, the whole outlook on affairs, the grouping of parties, all have encountered violent and tremendous changes in the deluge of the world. But as the deluge subsides and the waters fall, we see the dreary steeples of Fermanagh and Tyrone emerging once again. The integrity of their quarrel is one of the few institutions that have been unaltered in the cataclysm which has swept the world.'

The battle of the Border was fought so fiercely and so long precisely because it was difficult. Northern Ireland is still divided not only theologically, but also by a geographical/psychological line. But to draw that would be even more difficult than to decide on a Border which would meet with general satisfaction. Any generalisation about the boundaries of political sentiment is certain to be inaccurate. Speaking broadly, the eastern half of Northern Ireland contains the vast majority of the Protestant population, and a sufficiently small Catholic minority to make relations more relaxed than in the evenly-balanced western areas, particularly Fermanagh, Tyrone and parts of Londonderry.

It is in the west that animosities are strongest. It is there that most allegations about gerrymandering and discrimination in the allocation of houses and jobs are made. It is the western Unionists who give the whole Party its legacy of bitterness; it is the Nationalists from the same areas who have resisted most stubbornly any suggestion that Catholics should allow themselves to be integrated in the apparatus of the state.

The *de facto* segregation of large sections of the two communities, and particularly of working-class Protestants and Catholics, is primarily caused by the existence of two educational systems. Protestant children go to local authority schools; Catholics have insisted on exercising the right to educate their children in church schools. The State grants to these, though a subject of constant irritation to the more extreme Orange elements in the Unionist Party, have down the years been more generous than those received by Catholic schools in England. Because of the higher proportion of children who attend them, this was to be expected.

The damage caused by the separate primary and secondary schools is not unlike that done by the private sector in English education. A social apartheid exists in England between many of the people educated at preparatory and public schools on the one hand and state school pupils on the other; the same degree of apartheid exists between many Ulster Protestants and Catholics. Some Englishmen carry the separateness to Oxbridge and beyond; at least until recently, Queen's University, Belfast, has suffered from a self-imposed segregation among some of its students.

It may seem ludicrous for a London merchant banker solemnly to tell a researcher that although all his partners are public school men, most of the staff members came from grammar schools; it is no more and no less ludicrous and offensive when a Protestant suburbanite in Belfast says of his new Catholic neighbours: '*They're* getting in everywhere nowadays.' Hostility in each case is an index of unfamiliarity, and the educational systems are to blame.

A recent National Opinion Poll, published in the *Belfast Telegraph*, showed that young people were in favour of ending segregation in primary education by 65 per cent to 33; among Catholics the figures were 59/40. For secondary education there was a 70/28 margin in favour of mixed schools, and among Catholics the figure was higher, 74/25. The younger generation knows that it will never live together successfully until it learns together. Under the existing system, Protestant and Catholic children not only assimilate quite different views of Irish history and politics; they rarely even have the chance to hear the other side explained or discussed.

As a child I was fortunate to be friendly with two boys whose parents' marriages were 'mixed'. I thus had *entrée* to a small group of playmates which included several Catholics. It was, comparatively, a liberal education. I well remember, during the Second World War, the sensation caused in my home when I repeated a Catholic boy's casual quotation of the old saying that England's difficulty was Ireland's opportunity.

The war deepened the political and religious divisions in Ulster. Protestants and Catholics suffered alike in the air-raids. Belfast had more people killed in a single night—Easter Tuesday, 1941—than any other British city except London. Fire brigades from Dublin and other Southern cities came, lights blazing through the black-out, to succour the Northern capital. But the neutrality of the South was an irritant to the North, particularly as some Northern Catholics went out of their way to show support for Mr. De Valera. Belfast Celtic football supporters found a sure way to infuriate their Protestant rivals: they gave a Nazi salute when their team scored.

The segregation of the spirit which grows out of separate education and separate lives has an inevitable influence on political attitudes. Nationalist and Republican M.P.s have a real dilemma. Should they recognise and so enhance the respectability of a régime whose right to exist they deny? Should they compromise on oaths of allegiance, toasts to the Queen, Union Jacks and other symbols of Unionism? The dilemma has produced, at different times, Abstentionist M.P.s; some who were elected while in prison for I.R.A. offences; some who took their seats but would not form an official Opposition at Stormont; and some who would rarely speak on anything but Partition. This in turn has produced a governing party in which soundness on the constitutional issue wins a public representative more easy credit than intelligence, ability, fair-mindedness or the other virtues which earn candidates a parliamentary nomination in less single-minded political parties. And every time a Minister in Dublin, or a Labour M.P. in Lancashire with his eye on the Irish vote, speaks about Partition, he confirms some Unionists in their fortress mentality.

To the political generation before O'Neill's, the exploitation of the Border issue seemed as natural as breathing. They could argue, justly, that this was fundamental to politics, that it had more bearing on the living standards of Ulster people than any other decision, and that political opponents must say where they stood. Lord Brookeborough, O'Neill's predecessor, was a man of his generation. He had been through the Troubles. The Irish Republican Army threatened to kidnap one of his sons, then a child. In the bitterness of that period he was reported to have said that he would never employ a Catholic on his large estates in Fermanagh. The story haunted his subsequent political career.

It was his government which, in 1949, obtained from Lord Attlee a guarantee that Ulster would never be excluded from the United Kingdom without the consent of her Parliament. Brookeborough went to the country that year in what came to be called the Union Jack election. Catching the Northern Ireland Labour Party with its constitutional trousers down— indeed, split down the centre seam—he wiped out its representation at Stormont. It was a bitter election, with no solecism rejected, not even the importation of Sir Edward Carson's politically eccentric son, who was introduced to hysterical crowds in an attempt to stir up the feelings of the Home Rule days.

I remember attending one open-air Labour meeting in a

working-class area at which the candidate, trying to make his prepared speech on housing and unemployment, was constantly interrupted by shouts of 'where's the flag on your platform?' and 'are you going to sing "the King" at the end?' At last a leather-lunged man in a cloth cap, his patience tried beyond reason, turned and invited the hecklers to shut their bloody mouths until he could hear what the speaker was saying. It was an effective, though not a popular rebuke, and the meeting was allowed to end in sullen silence. The Labour candidate, incidentally, was an ex-serviceman of the First World War whose loyalty to Britain was not in doubt.

After the débâcle of 1949, the Labour Party committed itself to the maintenance of the British connection. The decision caused many of its Catholic members to split off and form Northern branches of the Irish Labour Party. The N.I.L.P. has had its ups and downs since then. In the early sixties it held four Stormont seats in the Belfast region, and seemed on the way to being an effective constitutional opposition. But it lost ground again in 1965, and the prospects for such a party will probably remain bleak while the Orange-Green division in society persists.

The sectarian nature of politics is often more obvious and more serious at local level than at Stormont. Occasionally it becomes high comedy. A Labour candidate for a Belfast Water Commissioners' election once stood in a ward in which he needed many Catholic votes if he was to succeed. Like many another man of the moderate Left, in his youth he had worked in the Belfast docks as a volunteer to load arms for Republican Spain. A gable wall still bore his requiem years after his unsuccessful attempt to join the Water Commissioners: 'What stand did ***** take for the Catholic Church on the Spanish question?' A man who opposed Franco was not to be entrusted by Catholics with supervision of their water supply.

Partisanship has its most serious effects in areas where local

Unionists are determined to maintain their majority by discriminatory allocation of houses and jobs. In the tightly contested areas of the West, local Unionist leaders—an American might bestow on them the pejorative title of satraps—make no secret of their methods of keeping their party in control. These are seen not as corruption, but as the essential defences of a difficult political fortress. One convivial St. Patrick's Day in a Nationalist-controlled area I heard a similar boast: not a single Protestant was employed by the local council.

What exacerbates feelings is that the debate over grievances like these, which affect people's standard of living, is often conducted against an irrelevant and explosive background of flag-waving, marching and posturing. Whenever the political pot in Ulster has seemed likely to go off the boil, an I.R.A. resurgence has reheated it. Their last campaign, between 1956 and 1962, caused the deaths of six policemen, injuries to thirty-four people, and damage costing £1 million. In the absence of violence, Southern politicians can usually be counted on to arouse the amusement and rage of Ulster Protestants by an assurance that they are being held down by a British Army of Occupation. Irish politics have often been conducted as fantasy on all sides, of course. But it was still a surprise that the Prime Minister of the Republic, Mr. Lynch, could be so out of touch with opinion in the North during the civil rights campaign. He enraged its leaders, and many Northern Nationalists, by a maladroit statement in London that Partition lay at the root of the trouble. His script might almost have been written by a Protestant extremist. But Mr. Lynch had an election coming.

While politicians have worried these Orange-and-Green bones for half-a-century, till all the meat might be thought to have gone, Northern Ireland has a problem which in any other part of the United Kingdom would dominate politics. It is unemployment. Ulster suffered with the other industrial areas of Britain in the Depression. War industries helped from 1939 till 1945, though the agricultural basis of the economy made the effects less decisive than elsewhere. Since the late forties, with employment in agriculture, shipbuilding and linen manufacture declining, the Government has known that it must attract new industries. Northern Ireland's is the problem of any fringe area in Britain, but accentuated by the physical and, more important, the psychological barrier of the Irish Sea. It sometimes seems that many British companies take their investment decisions according to how far away from Knightsbridge the managing director's wife can bear to live.

In full or near-full employment in Britain during the past twenty years it might have been expected that Ulster's pool of labour would be a powerful attraction to industrialists. With the long record of high unemployment grafted on to an industrial tradition, many of the workers are at once less choosey and easier to pay than their contemporaries in England, while not being hard to train. (On average Ulster workers earn £4 per week less than those in South-Eastern England.) Stormont was also well ahead of Whitehall in offering grants, loans and advance factories to attract new industry. It does not suffer from the remoteness of Government decision-makers that industrialists in outlying areas of Great Britain complain of. The visiting entrepreneur in Ulster often finds that the man he expected to be a distant bureaucrat turns out to be an intimate and helpful adviser and sorter-out of his problems.

Although the highest birth-rate and lowest death-rate in the British Isles, combined with the decline in traditional employment, has often seemed to leave Ulster running fast to keep in the same place, the drive for new jobs has been a success. Since 1945 the Government has helped 250 firms, giving work to 70,000 people, to establish themselves. This is more than one-third of the total employment in manufacturing, and it will rise to 100,000 when these companies reach full production. The scale of diversification is measured by the fact that in 1949, 55 per cent of manufacturing workers were in shipbuilding or textiles. Today the figure is only 36 per cent.

Yet Ulster, with 7 per cent unemployment, still has the worst figure in the United Kingdom. Some apologists say that in agricultural areas a practice called 'working and drawing' is prevalent. With variations, it means that a farmer employs men on a casual basis and pays them, without making a return. This allows them to augment their earnings by drawing unemployment benefit and perhaps supplementary benefit (the old National Assistance) as well. The fraud also saves the farmer money, for the wages he pays are smaller than normal.

Even if the figures in rural areas are inflated, however, unemployment and the poverty and frustration it causes are at the root of much community tension. Protestants and Catholics compete for too few jobs. Would the level of unemployment, sustained over many years, be tolerated in other parts of Britain? The question raises what seems to be an underlying weakness of devolution. When the Ulster Government was established, control of the area's economy—such as it was in pre-Keynsian days—remained with the British Government. It is still true that if Whitehall sneezes, Stormont is likely to catch pneumonia. Nothing has balked the campaign against unemployment more than the spasmodic deflationary policies of successive post-war governments at Westminster.

Now it is true that regions of high unemployment in Great Britain also suffer in these periods. It is also true that Stormont could probably have pursued a different taxation policy, had it wished, turning Northern Ireland into a tax haven like Jersey or the Isle of Man, and hoping to attract investment in that way. Wisely it decided not to. A major industrial area cannot exist on such flimsy foundations. Parity in public investment on roads, water supplies, drainage, housing, education and health services, and equality in social service benefits would have been impossible if the Ulster economy had not been bound tightly to that of Britain.

But the very existence of a separate government and legislature inevitably causes Ministers at Westminster to pass the buck on Ulster unemployment in a way that they cannot do about Scotland, the North-East and South Wales. Human nature being what it is, who can be surprised if it is the most intractable problems that politicians in London decide must be devolved? The financial help that Whitehall has given for Ulster development has been generous. But so has the help given to other areas in Britain that were blighted by the Industrial Revolution and the Depression. In each case it has been necessary help to catch up the leeway of inadequate social spending in the past. The North-East of England may be fortunate that it has no separate accounts in which the subsidy can be measured.

One of O'Neill's successes as Minister of Finance was to build up relationships with Treasury officials that have paid useful dividends since, when a motorway or a dry-dock has been needed. The most cheering development in Ulster at present is the transformation which is taking place in the physical environment: the building of the new university at Coleraine, the new city of Craigavon in Armagh, and the motorway network, as well as houses and schools. He also got on good enough terms with Labour leaders, after he became Prime Minister, to make sure that when Mr. Wilson's Government took office the generous financial treatment would continue. It would have been shameful if it had not; after Lord Attlee's Government went into opposition in 1951, a strong Labour group, which included Mr. Callaghan and Lord Robens (then a front-bench M.P.), had visited Belfast and produced a detailed blueprint on Ulster's economic difficulties. It is good to know that political memories are so long.

Whichever political party is in power at Westminster, however, a weakness of devolution is that it creates a client relationship between Belfast and London. To set Stanley Baldwin's jibe at Fleet Street on its head, it might be said that Stormont enjoys responsibility without real power, the prerogative of the eunuch of every age. To an extent, every side in the civil rights controversy has been appealing, through television screens, the Press and Parliament at Westminster, to British public opinion. This address to a jury that is only listening with half-an-ear is not a new development in Ulster politics. Over the years the province has been afflicted by many Friends of Ireland groups in England or Minutemen in the Unites States.

The other great failing of devolution has been that it has robbed Northern Ireland's representation at Westminster of its most talented men. In this generation, Terence O'Neill and Brian Faulkner, the Minister of Development, have the ability and personality to make their marks at Westminster. I am not convinced that, if Stormont had never existed, they and others might not have served the North of Ireland as well or better as its representatives and advocates in London. Did Wales gain or lose by having Lloyd-George and Bevan at Westminster instead of Cardiff?

But O'Neill's strength as a statesman was to take a situation which he must have found uncongenial, and mould it to his convictions and principles. He has the inestimable advantage which so many Ulster politicians lack of having experience of the world outside Ireland. This enables him to see Northern Ireland's problems in a wider context, and to escape from its stifling parochialism. Having lived out of Ulster before and during the war, he consciously set out during a political career which began in 1946 to learn a lot quickly. A spell at the Ministry of Health and Local Government under Mr. William Grant, a natural working-class politician, was a good beginning. He had a period as Deputy Speaker, which allowed him to study the vagaries of a small House of Commons. His tenure at Home Affairs was shorter than it might usefully have been: Lord Brookeborough asked him to take on the Ministry of Finance. There he extended the office, obtained a seat on the British delegation to the World Bank and other international conferences, and built up contacts which were to prove useful later.

A strong will for change was the guiding light of O'Neill's Premiership. He began as a young man looking afresh at ideas which older men had left unquestioned for forty years. He was a Kennedy, urgent for reform, after the Eisenhower years of Brookeborough. The mood came out in all sorts of ways. For years Stormont had convinced itself that the Northern Ireland trade union movement must not be recognised because it belonged to a Congress which was Dublin-based. O'Neill saw only that he could not get the unions' co-operation in economic planning unless he recognised their central body, the Northern Committee of the Congress. It was recognised.

He saw his principal task, however, as the healing of the age-old rift between Protestant and Catholic. Visits by a Unionist Prime Minister to Catholic schools, newspaper photographs of him standing with the Mother Superior of a convent offended old-line Unionists and won him enemies. The first meetings to take place between Prime Ministers of the two states in Ireland, though they marked an implicit recognition by Dublin of Stormont's right to exist, also stirred up the extremists.

It was undoubtedly the new Prime Minister's liberal attitudes, actions and speeches which brought out from under their stones these advocates of hatred and intolerance. The Reverend Ian Paisley probably regards himself as true heir to Craigavon's slogan, 'not an inch'. O'Neill would not contend with him for the inheritance. He was openly willing to go much further than an inch in an effort to bind up wounds which have weakened Northern Ireland for the whole fifty years of its existence.

Both men have their constituencies within the population of Ulster. Mr. Paisley speaks to elements among the extreme Protestants who would be content for Catholics to live permanently as an unintegrated and underprivileged group in the community. His supporters' intolerance of ideas they disagree with and of people they despise, their determination not to let those ideas be publicly expressed, lie behind much of the disturbance during the civil rights campaign.

O'Neill spoke a different language, though he tried to extend his message to the same people. He sought to enlist the spirit which has always enabled neighbours of different religion and politics to live together with greater kindliness and mutual self-help in Ulster than in many, or even most other parts of the world. He tried to persuade ordinary Ulstermen that they ought not to leave their humanity and friendliness outside on the doorstep when they enter the polling booth or council chamber.

At the height of the civil rights campaign, when protest had begun to deteriorate into riot and counter-riot, raising the spectre of the communal strife Ulster had known in the thirties, O'Neill made a broadcast. It was his supreme effort to appeal over the heads of political activists on either side to the common humanity of ordinary Protestants and Catholics. This produced an immediate and heart-warming response. Whatever coolness there might be in the Unionist Party to the Prime Minister's liberal policies, whatever doubts Catholic politicians might have about the pace of change, hundreds of thousands of ordinary citizens showed that they were bored, frightened or offended by the revival of old hatreds and feuds.

The Government had gone some way to meet the demands of the civil rights movement. A commission was set up to do something about Derry's economic distress, and the suspension of Derry Corporation's activities removed the anomaly of a Nationalist majority ruled by a Unionist local authority. An Ombudsman was to investigate grievances over government administration, and a points system was expected to produce a fairer allocation of council houses.

But O'Neill did not have enough support in his Party or Cabinet to promise the immediate introduction of another demand of the civil rights people, universal adult suffrage in council elections, and the disturbances in the streets continued. This issue is important less because of its likely political effects—for more Protestants than Catholics stand to gain the vote under the reform—but because of the light it casts on Unionist attitudes. The average Englishman or Scot who heard the chant of 'one man, one vote' on a television news bulletin probably believed for many months that Ulster M.P.s at Stormont and Westminster were being elected on some kind of rigged franchise. The damage to the reputation of Northern Ireland in Britain was immense. Yet rather than give way under pressure many Ulstermen were willing to suffer that misrepresentation and damage. It reflects a national stubbornness that is a vice rather than the virtue it was taken for when Northern Ireland was being founded.

By February 1969 O'Neill faced with schism in his Cabinet and Party, knew that he must have a fresh mandate, so he called a General Election. It was the most extraordinary campaign that even Ulster has witnessed, almost a coupon election. Opponents of the Prime Minister within the Unionist Party found themselves facing candidates called 'Pro-O'Neil Unionists'. O'Neill and many of his leading supporters had Paisleyite opponents. Young candidates from the civil rights movement challenged Unionists and Nationalists right across the country.

The result was deadlock. The polls confirmed the depressingly conservative nature of the Ulster situation which has been suggested in this preface: O'Neill was able to continue as Prime Minister for a time, but all except two or three of his opponents in the Unionist Party were returned also. As ever, the label 'Official Unionist' was enough to see most candidates safely home. Caligula's horse would have had no difficulty reaching Stormont once he obtained the Unionist nomination. The election produced neither a decisive mandate for reform, nor any kind of mandate against it. O'Neill's revolution, in spite of the response to his broadcast a couple of months previously, still lacked vigour at the grassroots.

It was lack of grassroots support in the Unionist Party itself which finally overwhelmed him at the end of April. Hundreds of thousands of Ulster people fervently want the new spirit he offered in government, but many of them were not the kind of people who could stomach local Unionist Associations or Orange Lodges. Ministers and M.P.s who personally supported his reforms came under more and more pressure from Paisleyites and other extremists in their constituencies. Even before the election one supporter had had the humiliation of seeing a crowd kneel in the street outside his suburban home and pray for him to repent the error of supporting the Prime Minister.

As the pressure from such people mounted, it became more difficult for O'Neill to sustain his majority within the Unionist Parliamentary Party; even more so in the Ulster Unionist Council and its Standing Committee. His last great act of courage as Prime Minister was to force the symbolic 'one man, one vote' through the Parliamentary Party by a handful of votes. It took several threats of resignation to carry the day. But in the process he lost his Minister of Agriculture through resignation. O'Neill soon decided that he had not enough support to carry on, and he convinced his closest friends that he must go quickly if he was not to take the whole liberal wing of the Unionist Party over the precipice with him.

Ironically, the man whose resignation as Minister of Agriculture proved the last straw for O'Neill succeeded him as Prime Minister. James Chichester-Clark immediately accepted a universal local government franchise as the decision of the Party, and promised a fresh reform to deal with discrimination and other abuses by local councils. But the Cabinet he formed, a depressing coalition of hard- and soft-liners, showed that the crusading years of the O'Neill era were over.

Why did it end? The real obstacle to the creation of a more tolerant Ulster society is not the existence of extremism, both in the Unionist and Republican camps. The working-class rabble-rousers of Sandy Row in Belfast or Bogside in Derry are a product of the society in which they have grown up and whose values they have never questioned. O'Neill's drive towards liberalism was hindered more by the pusillanimousness of the middle classes, the lack of a lead from business and professional men and the ordinary well-educated inhabitants of suburbia.

Honor Tracy once satirized Ireland's traditional attitude of 'Mind you, I've said nothing'. It exists in the North as well as the South. The reasons are easy to see. A political history shot through with bigotry and violence does not attract into public life men and women who would be happier to serve if they lived in a blander climate. Many educated people who might join Conservative, Labour or Liberal associations if they were in England are quickly bored by the narrowness they encounter in local Unionist or Nationalist organisations.

Both parties have as their *raison d'être* a single political issue. How can the discussions and the attitudes be other than narrow? The Unionist Party may be a wide political coalition, but it is often the extremists who make the most noise at local meetings. For moderate Protestants a decision to take part in politics raises the problem of whether to join the Orange Order, which any Unionist with serious political ambitions is expected to do. The Catholics have the frustration of belonging to parties which can never expect to form a government.

But even among ordinary electors 1969 showed too few supporters for change. The response of two groups of voters especially chilled the spirits of those who believe that Ulster's only future lies in reform. The large vote for Paisleyite candidates, and particularly that for Paisley himself against O'Neill in the Bannside Division of County Antrim, demonstrated that uncompromising and bigoted Protestantism is neither dead nor dying in parts of Ulster. Indeed, the reform policies that O'Neill fathered have produced their own reaction. Though the majority of Unionist voters seemed to be committed to a measure of change, those who want it to come quickly still have to persuade many thousands of Ulster Protestants of the need to change at all.

Catholic conservatism was equally in evidence at the polls. All the pious talk about the need to end sectarianism did not persuade many Catholics to vote for a Protestant—however tolerant his attitudes might be—if there was a Catholic's name on the ballot. It was an odd form of conservatism, this, very much with a small 'c'; for it must have caused many an elderly Catholic farmer to vote for young candidates whose affection for Trotsky was stronger than their loyalty to Pope Paul. But in an election where colour—orange or green—still counted most, it was enough for a candidate to be a cradle Catholic to get the Catholic vote. The same conservatism showed itself again in the Mid-Ulster by-election which brought Miss Bernadette Devlin to Westminster in April on a vote that split almost totally on sectarian lines.

If ever the sectarian basis of Ulster politics is to be ended and a normal system of alternating governments created, a re-alignment of the political parties seems the ineluctable first step. To my mind O'Neill's speeches are interesting because they lay the ground for an Ulster in which politics and religion could eventually be separated; in which two or more parties with both Protestants and Catholics in their membership and among their leaders could contend for office.

O'Neill said in his farewell broadcast: 'We could have enriched our politics with our Christianity, but far too often we have debased our Christianity with our politics.' It is a text which will endure even after its author has left the Premiership. A pessimist may conclude from the story of his downfall that rapid change in Ulster is impossible. Paradoxically, the truth may be that gradual change is even more difficult.

In conclusion, though perhaps I need hardly say it to anyone who has read this far, the views in this essay are my own. Many of them, particularly those critical of devolution as a principle of government, are unlikely to be shared by Terence O'Neill, or indeed by any of his colleagues or opponents. Stormont, most of them have probably concluded, is there to stay, whatever we may think of it, so they had better concentrate on making it work.

Claygate, Surrey
May, 1969.

CHAPTER I

Setting the Scene

It is not often that a Prime Minister, who spent over six years in office, can look back to a single speech as setting a keynote for his administration. It is rarer still that such a speech provided in itself much of the impetus for his elevation to the premiership. These comments can, however, be fairly made of the speech which Captain O'Neill, then Minister of Finance, made to the Pottinger Unionist Association on 29th November 1962. To understand the significance of what has become known as the 'Pottinger speech' it is necessary to take a brief view of the background. Northern Ireland's persistent unemployment problem had long been a source of anxiety to its own and to the United Kingdom Government. In 1961 the two Governments had established a Joint Working Party of officials to study the problem. When, in June 1962, the Report of this Working Party (advised by Sir Robert Hall) was presented to R. A. Butler, then Home Secretary, and to Lord Brookeborough, who had been Prime Minister of Northern Ireland for almost two decades, it was widely regarded by public opinion in Ulster as an austere and unpromising, if thorough, document. The Working Party had been unable to agree on proposals which would have any major impact upon the situation, and the prospect seemed to be a gloomy one.

Into this atmosphere, Captain O'Neill injected a speech of considerable vigour and basic optimism. In its emphasis upon self-

help, upon the need for management and labour-training, and upon the importance of vigorous promotion of trade and industrial investment, it gave the first public expression to many of the main themes of his premiership.

The 'Pottinger speech' began with a review of the existing incentives to economic development in Northern Ireland. It continued as follows:

We have achieved great things in the face of immense difficulties. We have already transformed Northern Ireland's economy from a narrowly-based to a broadly-based structure. We have held the line while old industries have faltered. But it is not enough. We must do more. We intend to do more.

The Hall Report is a great watershed in our affairs. It has given us a cold impersonal look at ourselves. It has tested the ability of the Imperial Government to help us in certain areas and met a negative response. Now we as a Government and those to whom we are responsible know where we stand. Very well then. We must now proceed with a three-pronged attack upon our problems, relying largely upon our own skill, determination and enterprise. What are these three routes by which we may advance? First by self-help. Secondly, by the full use of our advantages. Thirdly, by the development of unused resources.

'Self-help' means a great deal. Let us remember that when Britain led the world in industrial development it was not because of any unique natural endowment. True, there were coal and iron, but in today's world we see that many countries in every part of the world had far greater mineral wealth. These isolated off-shore islands owed their lead to the inventiveness of Watt, Stephenson, Crompton, Priestley—to men who were not just 'thinkers' but 'do-ers'. There is almost no disadvantage of location which cannot be overcome if you can invent something new which the world wants, and make

it supremely well. Nor is that all. Any careful student of international industry can determine emerging product trends.
Why is it that exciting new products being made in Northern
Ireland—with a few honourable exceptions—have to come to
us from the outside? True, some projects need immense capital
resources which are not easily accumulated. Others require
secret technological know-how which is in a few hands. Yet,
even taking all these factors into account, is ours a sufficiently
daring, a sufficiently inventive society to succeed?

We need, as I said, to be a Province of 'do-ers'. We need
people who will submit themselves to the discipline of thought
and action as readily as they indulge themselves in the luxury
of criticism. Are those who cry loudest about the lack of capital
prepared to invest in Ulster Bonds? Are those in industrial
management who cry ruin at every moment of difficulty really
doing their utmost to boost productivity and maximise sales?
I believe that throughout the length and breadth of Ulster
there are companies with unrealised export potential. How
many of our factories are involved in production with a high
labour cost, and yet have never looked into the possibility of
selling to countries such as the United States, where labour is
paid about three times as much? I would like to see a business
mission from Ulster scouring the length and breadth of North
America, and really putting our exports on the map. If my
diplomatic and commercial contacts from three recent visits to
the United States are considered of any use, I would be prepared to accompany such a mission myself. This is normal
Whitehall practice where people like Lord Rootes tour North
America accompanied by a Minister.

And let me say a word to the ordinary Ulsterman at his
loom or lathe. Self-help means *you*. At present the average
Ulsterman earns four guineas a week less than his counterpart in London and the South-East of England—not, mark
you, because basic wage rates are generally much lower. Some

of this differential is due to the different types of industry and levels of skills required and some to the wage drift brought about by the scarcity of labour in some areas. But there is a school of thought, the 'I'm all right, Jack' school of thought, which says 'Let's hold on to our individual jobs whatever happens. If the total demand slackens off, let's work a little less hard and spread it around. Let's keep the level of training and apprenticeship down, so that there won't be too much competition'. But attitudes such as these will, in the long run, reduce employment, not maintain it. They will make our industries less and less competitive in world markets. If we are going to raise our earnings we are going to have to work a little harder to overcome our economic disadvantages. This is not a prescription for sweated labour, it is simple economics. Self-help for the Ulster worker may well consist of convincing his fellow employees in his factory, or his brothers in his Union, that there is no other road to prosperity than the road to hard work.

Let me tell you a story. From time to time American industrialists come to Ulster when they are considering setting up a factory somewhere in the United Kingdom. Naturally they are keen to see other American factories which are already in production, especially if they are in a similar line of business. A year or two ago such an American party arrived in Northern Ireland and asked to see a particular factory. But these American businessmen never went inside for their discussion, for on arrival, they found the place plastered with 'Yanks go home'. They did. And we never saw them again.

Now I know that there are always two sides to a dispute. But we cannot afford to have the reputation of being a difficult labour area, on top of all our other problems.

Certain unions in Northern Ireland have considerable power. To exercise this power to bring a great industry to a standstill is a great responsibility to take. It merely adds one more hazard to the list of hazards which British, Continental, or American firms feel they face here. I appeal to all Unions to weigh well the possible results of actions whose effects can never be confined to the single firm against which they are directed.

So much for 'self-help'. Let each of us look into his conscience and ask himself whether he can do more for Ulster. Now I turn to the question of 'full use of our advantages'. I have already described the generous nature of our present aids to industry. Now I say this in addition with all the responsibility of my office as Minister of Finance. If there is any case of an industrial project in which an industrialist claims that he can get better terms somewhere else in the United Kingdom, then I will personally go into the possibility of improving those terms—as I have done on several occasions before. I will support the Ministry of Commerce in a flexible approach to any specific negotiation.

Many hurdles have to be overcome before a firm finally decides to come to Northern Ireland. After an initial investigation the firm concerned often consults its own experts as to whether the whole proposition is feasible; this causes delay and may entail expense. When these problems reach a more advanced stage of consideration, the management concerned which may itself be involved in a move then inevitably starts wondering whether they really want to come on a personal basis. Can they face leaving London? Will their families be happy in Northern Ireland? How will children, used to a London school get on at an Ulster school? While, last but by no means least, there is anxiety about leaving the golf club or the sailing club which provides the Manager's chief leisure, amusement and sport. At this stage he should have it stressed to him that Ulster can provide him with the best golf and sailing within the United Kingdom at a reasonable price. For an American who has to cross the Atlantic in any case it makes little difference to him whether he comes to the home of the Scotch-Irish or the Scotch!

I was talking in America to the head of one of the most successful businesses in New England. His British subsidiary is split between London and Belfast. So far as he was concerned he would really have preferred that the entire enterprise should be shifted to Northern Ireland. But he told me that the London resistance to such a move was an insuperable stumbling block. When people talk about the attraction of industry they do so in an impersonal manner. But often it is these personal considerations which, at the heels of the hunt, decide the location of the firm. Anything which can be done to get a firm over the final hurdle either of its 'feasibility studies' or its personal problems is, in my view, of the utmost importance.

Above all we must concentrate upon the development of unused resources. Let us face the hard fact that in the modern world the worker—particularly the middle-aged worker—thrown on the labour market without skills is increasingly unlikely to be re-employed. Our first priority, therefore, must be to step up dramatically the whole tempo of labour training, not just to create new skills. And here again self-help is going to be a vital element. We must ask both management and labour to take a broad view of the situation. We must ask employers to look beyond the immediate foreseeable requirements of their own business. We must persuade unions that the interests of labour as a whole demand that we discard restrictive attitudes to apprenticeship practices and labour training. We have already begun to take action with a limited scheme for additional training in the engineering industry. I hope that when additional proposals are formulated, both labour and management will be co-operative with us. And again I say, as Minister of Finance, money will not be allowed to stand in the way of developments in this direction. Even the Hall Committee, with its divisions on many major issues, acknowledged that this was a direction in which we could make real progress.

While I have no doubt that labour training is one of the most important things we could do, nevertheless the reverse side of the medal would be management training. When I was interviewed by Mr. Michael Shanks of the *Financial Times* a few months ago, this author of *The Stagnant Society* who later wrote such excellent articles on Northern Ireland, suggested that this was a most important aspect of industrial development which was often overlooked by both governments and industries. It is to be assumed that an industry which has recently expanded into Northern Ireland would probably ensure that its new management was fully equipped and instructed. But it might be that older industries would find it valuable to be able to take advantage of some such scheme. Once again I would certainly press such a scheme in London if that proved necessary, and if it were decided that there was a general demand for it.

Earlier this year I made a speech in which I said that we should discard the old concept of step-by-step as having served its purpose. If you start a race with a handicap you are going to have to run faster on some part of the course if you are to catch up. This is tacitly acknowledged in our 'leeway' expenditure, under which as I have shown we have developed social services at the fastest rate in the United Kingdom. We must now strike out equally boldly in the direct economic field. Give me a really dramatic scheme of labour training supported both by management and labour, and I will fight for its acceptance in London with every ounce of my strength and energy. This is Covenant year. We can hear the voices of our forbears—amongst them that of my own father—echoing down the corridors of time, with the cry 'We *will* be citizens of the United Kingdom. We will accept no less'. And we were not afraid, in those days, to press our case with vigour, and with the support of great Englishmen—F. E. Smith, Long, Bonar Law. Today we must send back an answering cry 'We will be *full* members of the United Kingdom. We will accept no less'. Did Beveridge write his report only for Englishmen? Is 'full employment' to be an empty promise for those of us who live on the frontiers of the United Kingdom? This Government will do what it can. This Government will do what it must. But the great powers of control of the economy, the ultimate purse strings, the final instruments of fiscal and economic policy—these are in London, not in Belfast. I welcome, therefore, the Chancellor's more generous treatment of capital investment in industry: this reflation of the economy should start a tide whose ripples will reach this shore. But far, far more radical measures may be needed if the United Kingdom is not to become a 'concentrated economy'—a tree bearing rich fruit in the Midlands and South-East, but with its other branches withering away. There is a long-term trend in motion here, and not a healthy one. The United Kingdom needs the Ulsterman, the Scot, the Sturdy Durham miner, the tough Merseyside factory worker, if it is to continue to be the great, rich, diverse nation it has always been.

I spoke of allies in our struggle in 1912. I believe we have allies today, in every part of the United Kingdom which protests against the 'concentrated economy'. The worthy efforts of the Board of Trade to steer industrial development to Northern Ireland and to other unemployment areas must not be relaxed. They must be strengthened. Every expansion of industry in the London area—adding to its traffic and housing chaos—which could have been located elsewhere is a blow to our hopes. As for ourselves, we must proceed, not to construct buttresses, but to dig foundations. A dramatic scheme of labour training will permanently improve our attractiveness to industry.

Apart from labour, are we using our other resources fully

and efficiently? Do we, for example, seek diversification quickly enough when staple product lines begin to falter in world markets? Do we spend enough on advertising? Do we as individuals when we go outside emphasise its opportunities, rather than bewail its problems?

Ever since I came to the Ministry of Finance I have always made a point of seeing that money was made available for mineral exploration. A country which has comparatively few natural resources cannot afford to neglect any possibilities which may exist of discovering some hitherto hidden mineral wealth. With this in view the Geological Survey people have made an aeromagnetic survey and also a gravity survey of the area. Apart from the great variety of rocks found within its border, there are unfortunately great sheets of basalt covering wide areas of Ulster and this presents a serious obstacle to deep exploration. I will, however, certainly see that money is still forthcoming to continue these investigations.

Understandably people have felt that we should make the maximum use of any raw materials we may possess. It is gratifying therefore that Meat Processing is now getting under way at various centres. For the Deep-Freeze and the 'can' now form a vital part of food distribution, especially with the growth of the self-service store and the supermarket. Sometimes when one sees how peat has been developed in Eire one regrets that hitherto no one has come forward to carry out a similar development here. It is a tragedy that quasi government organisations are always equated in people's minds with the difficult times through which the U.T.A. has passed. Few people realise, however, that those difficulties were largely created by saddling the Authority with the burden of the G.N.R. But it should be remembered that another board—the Electricity Board—unhampered by such difficulties, has been able to achieve considerable success and in consequence to borrow on the London Market along with all the other vast British undertakings.

Above all let us keep a sense of proportion about our problems. Here we are a small, well developed, rather progressive little country, with social services second to none, where no person need go hungry. We have ready access to the richest most rapidly growing market in the world. Production is rising and employment is not far off its all-time peak. There are more cars, more television sets, more appliances than ever before. Ulster has always been a proud place where people have stood against the world. This is not the time and we are not the men to let our problems break our spirit. If one way is barred to us, we must take another. But let us not, in a moment of bitterness, forget all the progress we have made, in co-operation with our friends in London, for over forty years. It is easier to climb the mountain from the plateau than from the valley. We have been climbing—slowly, unspectacularly perhaps—but nonetheless climbing for more than four decades. If we look back to that distant point from which we have ascended, we will have the courage to press on to the summit.

(*Pottinger Unionist Association, 29th November 1962*)

In February 1963, under the influence of the most severe weather conditions for many years, the unemployment rate in Northern Ireland mounted to the alarming level of 11·2 per cent. The following month, amidst mounting public concern about the economic situation, the long premiership of Lord Brookeborough came to an end when ill-health forced him to retire. In this difficult situation, the ruling Unionist Party turned to the man whose urgent call for self-help and self-reliance had been made less than four months before. In March 1963, Terence O'Neill became Prime Minister of Northern Ireland.

The 'Pottinger speech' had already defined many of his aims in public life. Now, on 5th April 1963, at the Annual Meeting of the Ulster Unionist Council, he developed additional objectives for his new administration.

The growth industries of the next fifty years will not be at all similar to those industries in which Britain experienced the world's first Industrial Revolution. They depend not so much upon access to great reserves of coal or iron-ore, as upon intensive research and development, a high level of education throughout the community, and the right kind of social and economic environment. Nature does not create these facilities, but with determination and foresight we can do so.

Our task will be literally to transform the face of Ulster. To achieve it will demand bold and imaginative measures. Let me quote to you—because I believe it hits the nail on the head—a passage from the Belfast Regional Plan prepared by Sir Robert Matthew. 'The whole industrial (and therefore social) future of Northern Ireland is' he says 'balanced, at the present time, on a fine edge. The task is to concentrate all efforts on assisting the economy to respond to long-term as well as short-term measures; and that, from experience in progressive countries, is where town and country planning can play a constructive part. I wish to emphasise this practical point. The total image presented to the modern industrialist has many facets, but outward appearances are becoming more and more important.'

In Belfast and other cities there are thousands of tiny terrace houses. The people who live in those houses are the salt of the earth—they are the muscle and sinew not only of Ulster industry but of much of our social and political life. When we think of 1912 we may remember first Carson, Craig, Bonar Law. But it was the fathers of these people, in their thousands and tens of thousands, who made Northern Ireland a vigorous reality. Go down one of these little streets and you will be struck at once by the pride and self-reliance of the people, shown in a polished door-knocker, a well-scrubbed step or a bowl of flowers in the window. But I say to you today that these little streets, these cramped houses, this environment without trees, without grass, without a view beyond the nearest factory chimney is not good enough for this day and age.

What has this to do with economic progress? A great deal. The point is that only unskilled labour is trapped in the net of immobility; the skilled man, the technologist, the scientist can expect to be in demand in many places provided the economy of the nation as a whole is reasonably buoyant. He will select his job partly on the basis of its financial rewards and its interest to him, but also on his assessment of what an area offers to his family as a place in which to live, to be educated, to enjoy leisure. Why is it that the population drift into London and the South-East has acquired such momentum? Partly at least because the kind of key employee required by such new growth industries as electronics wants to live the kind of full, satisfying life which he believes can be found there. And because a dozen or twenty key people can easily be attracted to such a location, all the other hundreds or thousands of new jobs requiring a lower degree of skill are also created there.

That is why I don't believe we should accept for Ulster a 'second-best' or 'also-ran' status. We must be leaders as often as we are followers. The Matthew Plan, to which I have already referred, suggests a way in which we may catch the imagination of the world. Think of it—a great new modern city of 100,000 in mid-Ulster, planned to be a complete contrast to the accumulation of decades of haphazard development elsewhere in the Province.

What is our policy? What is our programme? How is the future to be built? First, we must become a participating rather than a spectator society. For some, that participation will be political. Don't just criticize the Government and the Party from the outside. Join it, work to make it better, lend some of your time and talents to local politics. In our cities, town and rural areas there are a thousand useful things to be done under the guidance of men and women of energy. Too many people are dazzled by the allure of politics at a high level. They would rather make a speech at the United Nations, to which no one other than the interpreters may listen, than work quietly with minimum publicity to bring better education, better health and welfare services or improved water supply to their own neighbours. It's all part of a curious inferiority complex which has grown up in Ulster. We have got to achieve a tremendous improvement of morale. If, in our political and parliamentary activities, we show a lack of vigour and imagination, it will have a gradual and insidious effect upon the calibre of those who enter our public life. Able people will serve the State, whether at party, political or administrative level, only if they believe that they will be able to make some real contribution to the life of Ulster, some real impact upon its major problems.

Secondly, we must participate fully at the working level. This means the acceptance of responsibilities which must outweigh any sectional interest. Those who own and control industries must realize that even a family business is not entirely a personal possession, but to some extent a trust to which others have contributed. At the management level, our programme for progress demands a growing acceptance of higher management standards, including formal management training. It demands, too, a great deal more co-operative management within Ulster. A huge international company such as Du Pont points the way by its purchase every year of millions of pounds worth of goods and services from other Ulster companies. Most firms are consumers as well as producers. They owe it to the community to explore carefully the availability of Ulster-made supplies, and the Ministry of Commerce would, I know, be only too delighted to assist them. At the employee level, I ask the patriotic Ulster worker to keep before him the needs and the problems of his Province, as well as his own interests and those of his Trades Union brethren. The Ulster worker is almost our only, and certainly our best, raw material. He is capable of working as hard, as skilfully and as productively as anyone in the world. It is the knowledge of this fact—more than all the advance factories, cash grants, loans or other Government aid—that has developed in Ulster more than 170 new industries now in production. The best sort of Trades Union leader—a man who works for ever-increasing productivity and for growing profits in which his members will share—such a man is one of the key figures in our blue-print for the future.

Our programme to change the face of Ulster takes many forms. It is a new motorway driving deeper into the Province. It is a new airport which will match our position as the busiest domestic air centre in Britain outside London. It is a new hospital in Londonderry—the most modern in the British Isles. It is new laboratories and research facilities at Queen's to carry us to the frontiers of existing knowledge, and beyond. It is the replacement of derelict slums by modern housing estates. It is the steady containment of tuberculosis. It is our new National Museum and Folk Museum. And again it is worth quoting Sir Robert Matthew as an outside observer. 'Northern Ireland has much to offer; a growing population; available skilled and experienced labour or unskilled labour quick to learn—surely an asset of greater value today . . . ; space to expand at very low cost; convenient access to good ports; no shortage of water; an accessible and attractive countryside offering a great variety of interests for tourist and for leisure activities; roads still uncrowded for motoring.' 'All this' he says 'adds up to a type of environment potentially of great value in the world of tomorrow, a type of environment becoming increasingly rare, and therefore more valuable, in Europe where past industrialization has been allowed or has allowed itself more and more to destroy natural amenity. Once destroyed, it is difficult or impossible to replace. The seamy side of industrialism has not, so far, overwhelmed the general environment of Northern Ireland: this is a factor to put at the top of the list in its favour.'

(Ulster Unionist Council, 5th April 1963)

CHAPTER 2

Unionism

As Leader of the Ulster Unionist Party, O'Neill frequently set out to define, or indeed to re-define its nature, organisation, principles and policies. The following represent a reasonable selection from his many speeches on this theme.

O'Neill has also been conscious of the need to make the philosophy and policies of his Party attractive to the younger generation.

I want, if I can, tonight to put the case for Unionism in a way which will be relevant to your generation, without slogans, catch-cries or polemics. A modern political party has to write its record in something more enduring than chalk on a wall. And really one of the obstacles in the way of serious discussion of politics in this country is the mass of sentiment, emotion and mere ancient history which has grown on everything like so much ivy.

I start from the basis that any government must offer men more than a roof over their heads, a book to read and food in their stomachs. When we think of the ultimate in orderly and well-regulated societies, our minds turn to thoughts of *1984* and *Brave New World*. Where does the dividing line lie? Good government, I would suggest, is that which looks to the dignity of man, as well as to his needs.

46

Now the fundamental purpose of Unionism, as you know, is to preserve a parliamentary union with Great Britain unbroken, as far as we are concerned, since the start of the nineteenth century. Those who oppose us will attempt to convince you that Northern Ireland is some kind of last-minute expedient. It is well to remember that this area has been within the United Kingdom since the days of Napoleon. It is also well to remember that both Churchill and Eisenhower doubted whether the last war could have been won without Ulster.

Some people attach little importance to the question of nationality. They may regard nationalism as a passing phenomenen, and national pride as a bar to greater world unity. Others see the nation solely as a kind of paymaster, worthy of support only for what one gets out of it. For these people, 'Ask not what your country can do for you' is a meaningless phrase in a materialistic world. But the sort of Unionism in which I believe sees more in our ancient link with Britain than an historical accident or an economic convenience. He sees in it a chance to play a useful and rewarding part in events far beyond the local scene. I know well that your generation has a deep antipathy to the idea of War—that you have no sympathy with anything which smacks of militarism. But granted all that, are you not proud to be part of a nation which twenty years ago triumphed over the most evil tyranny the world has ever known? A nation, morever, which then proceeded, with magnanimity and good judgment to convert its imperial heritage into a commonwealth of independent states? And let us remember to whom these same states, with a revealing gesture of confidence, turn when their new-found responsibilities weigh heavily upon them.

I stress this aspect first because I believe our besetting sin is our attachment to the parish pump. As a part of Britain, we keep our 'window on the world' wide open; we run little risk of falling into the fallacy of 'ourselves alone'.

Here at home in Ulster our basic policy may be simply stated. We want everyone to make a contribution to prosperity; and equally we want everyone to benefit from that prosperity. In that context I think the time may be ripe for me to say a few words about the unfortunate divisions in our society. They are often exaggerated and exacerbated, for not very worthy motives. Currently, they are being blown up into an organized pre-Election stunt. But it is true that they exist, and that they hamper and harm us. We have got to realize that in our Province there are many people with opinions widely different from our own—opinions strongly and sincerely held. Our object as Unionists must be to convince those who are now in opposition to us that their own ultimate best interests lie in the maintenance of Northern Ireland as a part of the United Kingdom. That is not a task which can be accomplished overnight. In the meantime, it is vitally important that we should think and speak of each other with charity and understanding. There are, however, certain principles which we must maintain.

Our opponents are nowadays extremely glib with such emotive terms as 'apartheid'. Where there is 'apartheid' in our society it comes almost entirely from a voluntary separation from the mainstream of our public and social life. This starts at an early age with the insistence that certain children cannot attend State schools. It is a most unhealthy basis for any society. How much happier this Province would be if Ulstermen of all persuasions could meet and mix and discuss matters as readily as they do in this University. But it is not the state which bars anyone from any of its institutions; the act of isolationism comes from another quarter.

I have said that it is our aim to convince everyone that their ultimate best interests lie within the United Kingdom. As Minister of Finance I came to know that we are utterly dependent on London for the maintenance of our British standard of living. And I assert that anyone who suggests that we could forge ahead industrially without our London connections would qualify for inclusion in one of Lewis Carroll's books.

There is no other financial or economic setting than the one which we at present enjoy which would permit us to plan for the sort of growth we now contemplate. This is not just a question of nationalism. We are not concerned with changing the face of Ulster and neglecting its heart. The plain fact is that all our other plans will be meaningless unless we can assure a decent standard of living. Quite simply it is a question of priorities. We cannot afford to conduct our affairs in the modern world in a haphazard way, indulging in a kind of political Micawberism—the hope that 'something will turn up'. Never before has the Government played such an active role in Ulster life.

(*Queen's University Unionist Association, 13th February 1964*)

Another major theme has been the need to move away from a mainly defensive basis of politics, and to develop a programme calculated to appeal to the widest sections of the community.

When Northern Ireland came into being, those people like Craig and Pollock and Dawson Bates, who had striven to maintain inviolate the unity of the United Kingdom, were faced unwillingly with the appalling task of turning a Province into a State, and of constructing here the whole apparatus of government and Parliament. Even at that time, it was a daunting task; but how would they have regarded it, if they had been able to look into the future and observe the trend which has since transformed the business of government? They set about their work in an atmosphere still largely based on *laissez-faire*. How could they have foreseen the complexities of the Welfare State, the involvement of the Government in

D
49

almost every aspect of the community's life, the immense burdens involved in modern administration?

In any case, the Ulster politics of those early years had a certain robust straightforwardness about them. If you are under heavy attack, the only thing to do is to defend. Our forefathers fought to base Ulster firmly, and they succeeded.

But now the whole atmosphere has changed. We face a world rapidly being transformed by science and technology, and in which a single development programme may demand as much finance as the whole of one of our earlier Budgets.

O'Neill, in emphasizing a forward-looking face of Unionism, has always been conscious of its history.

In our Parliament Buildings you will find a table, acquired when I was Minister of Finance, which is used by us for great occasions. Two recent Prime Ministers of the United Kingdom and a Prime Minister of Canada have sat down at that table. But its history is much longer and more significant than that—for it was upon that table that the Act of Union was signed in 1801. When, prior to appointment as a Minister, a Member of our Parliament is sworn as a member of the Privy Council of Northern Ireland, he holds in his hand a Testament used at the swearing of members of the Privy Council in Ireland ever since 1801. These things are history, but they are also symbolism. They demonstrate that the Union is not a thing of any decade or generation, but an enduring part of British history. Castlereagh and Canning, Palmerston and Peel, Gladstone and Disraeli—all of them have sat in Parliament with Members from Ulster constituencies. The Ulster Volunteers, the Covenant, the Government of Ireland Act, and the Ireland Act of 1949: all are part of a coherent pattern —a demonstration of the will and determination of the people of Ulster to remain within the United Kingdom.

Let no one in Ireland, North or South, no one in Great Britain, no one anywhere make the mistake of thinking that, because there is talk of a new Ulster, the Ulster of Carson and Craig is dead. We are building, certainly; but we build upon their foundations. And from that rock, no threat, no temptation, no stratagem will ever shake us. We stand four-square upon it.

But it is not enough, I would suggest to you, just to be part of the United Kingdom. We want to be a *progressive* part of that Kingdom. We want to secure for our people the full fruits of this great nation's prosperity. It must be our aim to demonstrate at all times, and beyond any possible doubt, that loyalty to Britain carries its reward in the form of a fuller, richer life.

(*Ulster Unionist Council, 30th April 1965*)

The major test of O'Neill's new emphasis came with the General Election of November 1965. In a major swing the Unionist Party substantially improved its already strong position. The Prime Minister's considered comment came in the following March, again at the Annual Meeting of the Ulster Unionist Council.

I was able to learn a great deal, at first hand, of the spirit of the people of Ulster. I found them less concerned with brooding about the past than with planning for the future. I found how facile is much of the talk about 'the divisions in our society', because in so many matters the hopes and aspirations of the great majority of our people are as one. I found them concerned with housing, and impressed with our plans for a further acceleration in house construction; concerned with jobs, and impressed by the pace and vigour of our new industries campaign; concerned with education, and impressed with the new educational opportunities being created every day. These are the things which occupy the minds of people today. They want to work together for these sensible and desirable aims.

(Ulster Unionist Council, 4th March 1966)

But 1966 was also a year of threatening portents, as Republicans celebrated the Fiftieth Anniversary of the Easter Rising of 1916, with an inevitable reaction from other sections of the community. In addressing the annual Party Conference, O'Neill found it necessary to warn against insularity and extremist attitudes.

In the long term, there is no future in a modern democracy for the advocates of extreme courses. A McCarthy or a Goldwater may have his brief hour of seeming ascendancy. But sooner rather than later, the great mass of people seek a middle ground. I believe it also to be true that there is little future today for a Party whose appeal is exclusive, and that it would be out of date to seek the support of a single class in an increasingly classless society.

Above all, we have to realize how much the world has changed around us. Universal education has made people aware of other standards than those of their immediate surroundings. Mass communications have made light of all the obstacles of time and space.

Today, we are aware of the world about us. But remember also that the world is aware of us. The luxury of insularity, of believing that we could take account only of the Northern Ireland point of view, is one we can no longer afford. If a great nation like the United States finds that isolationism is an impossible doctrine in the modern world, how much less can it be possible for us?

This applies most obviously to physical conditions. If we had not worked to create high standards, the incursion of new industry from Great Britain, North America and the Continent would not have occurred. Poverty and misery would have been our constant companions, as they were all too often in pre-War days. There may be many here who can still remember those times of massive unemployment, when barefoot children walked the streets of Belfast.

I give you this assurance today; from whatever quarter attacks upon us may come, we will resist them. The Government of Northern Ireland in the Twenties and Thirties faced appalling problems of physical violence and economic distress. By sheer determination they survived, and handed on to us the means of achieving better things. Now that we are making real progress, now that our people are sharing in ever-growing prosperity, now that increasing numbers from every background are realizing the benefits of the British connection —now is not the moment to interfere with the development of Northern Ireland. Let us rather re-double our efforts and concentrate our full energies upon building a finer society and a more prosperous economy in our native Ulster. Let us so serve our Province and our Nation that our children will say: this decade was the turning-point in our affairs: this was the time at which Ulster really broke through to British prosperity and British affluence.

(Unionist Party Conference, 29th April 1966)

In spite of O'Neill's cautionary words, the year 1966 did not pass without unhappy incidents. In November, the Prime Minister warned of their possible impact upon British public opinion.

Why is Northern Ireland a part of the United Kingdom today? Because the generation of the Ulster Covenant were courageous and determined, certainly. But of itself this would not have been enough. We survived a difficult period because a substantial proportion of the British people were at all times convinced of the justice of our cause. Carson and Craigavon were founders of Ulster, and we rightly honour them still.

But so also were many of the great British politicians of the day, and countless masses of the British people to whom any idea of coercing loyal Ulster was repugnant. We could not then, and we could not now 'go it alone'. The Union which we exist to preserve has two partners, and we are much the weaker of them. There can be no room in Unionist philosophy for a kind of loyalist Sinn Fein which would turn its back upon British opinion.

The events of 1966 have turned an intense and curious scrutiny upon us. And as we stand in this spot-light it remains as true now as it was over half a century ago that we must have the understanding and support of a substantial proportion of the British people. That is why we must condemn recent extremist activities which would not be supported by any of the British political parties or even by a single British M.P. Of course we cannot please everyone. There are certainly strong Southern Irish forces in Great Britain, with spokesmen in Parliament, who seek nothing less than the reunification of Ireland. We cannot please that section of opinion, and we are not going to try.

But the ordinary, decent Englishman, Welshman or Scot has an innate sense of justice and fair play. He will judge us on our merits. If we show him that we are pulling our full weight in the economic struggles of Britain; if we can demonstrate that behind all the talk about 'discrimination' is a warm and genuine community spirit; if we can demonstrate that we seek the advantages of British citizenship only because we bear the same burdens—then the voices of criticism will fall increasingly upon deaf ears.

If, on the other hand, we show again the picture of strife and squabble which has disfigured 1966, our staunchest friends may fall away from us. We must make sure that 1967 is a constructive year, upon which all our people will be able to look back with pride. The dark clouds of an economic storm lie ahead of us; if we are to keep the ship of prosperity on its course we must not allow ourselves to be distracted.

I do not want Ulster to change its nature, but rather to show again its best face to the world—the face of decent, hard-working, self-reliant people, playing a part in modern Britain of which they and their fellow-citizens 'across the water' can be equally proud.

(*Mid-Armagh Unionist Association, 19th November 1966*)

At all times, O'Neill has been anxious to indicate the relevance of Unionism in an age of change, and to illustrate the need for truly broad-based support. Thus, in January 1967, at Bally-money:

The times are changing, and will not wait for us. Unless we move with them we shall be left behind. We must make progress—economically, politically, socially, culturally—if we are not to fall behind and risk everything for which our forefathers fought and worked. What do the people of England today— what, indeed, do our own young people—know or care of Ulster's courageous and colourful past? We will be judged in Ulster, we will be judged elsewhere by what we are and what we hope to become.

Our work is not a dreary effort of plans and blue-prints and statistics. Forget jargon words like 'infrastructure' or 'community relations'. Rather keep before your eyes a vision of an Ulster which—if we will and work for it—can be. An Ulster whose superlative roads will bring an end to the comparative isolation in which parts of our Province have lived since time immemorial, bringing to them new prosperity and new hope. An Ulster in which our economic growth will keep pace with a growing population, providing satisfying and useful work for all. An Ulster in which slums will be at an end, and in which every home—however small—will be one of which a family can be proud. An Ulster in which every child has an equal opportunity to reach the top. Above all, an Ulster in which these material benefits will create such a spirit that our constitutional position will cease to be an issue in politics.

I tell you most earnestly and most sincerely that all these things are possible if we take the right road; if, in the finest traditions of Unionism, we regard change as our ally. But there is another possibility, another choice. We could retreat into some fortress mentality of our own, resisting all change, suspicious of every forward-looking idea, hostile and resentful of all who disagree with us. Make no mistake of where that road will lead us: to economic, to social, to political ruin, to a fatal breach in the ties of sympathy which have always bound us to the British people. This is a democracy. The choice is ours, to make freely. But as long as I am in a position to give a lead, I will urge the course which alone will keep our Province safe and strong.

(*North Antrim Unionist Association, 23rd January 1967*)

Moreover, O'Neill has never been slow to point out that, since Unionism's primary purpose is to support the union between Great Britain and Northern Ireland, there must be a willingness to make sacrifices for it. Thus, he used these words to the Area Conference of the British Legion.

We in Northern Ireland hear a great deal about the word 'loyalty'. But it is worthwhile to ask the question: what lies behind the display of the Union Jack and the other outward signs of our attachment to Queen and country? I am one of those who believe that patriotism is better demonstrated than proclaimed. For much of the time—and let us face up to this—Ulster's attachment to Britain is of great benefit to us. It guarantees our standard of living; it makes it possible for us to develop here all the services of a modern industrial state.

It is easy to be loyal, when the rewards of loyalty are so material and so self-evident.

But patriotism, like marriage, demands a loyalty to country which is 'for better for worse; for richer, for poorer; in sickness and in health'. If it provides benefits, it also expects sacrifices. And I greet all the delegates here today as Ulstermen who have shown their willingness to make such sacrifices.

1966 was a year of many different events—some happy, others tragic—but one day in particular will always remain in my memory. On 1st July, in the presence of a distinguished company, I pronounced the familiar words 'We will remember them' at Thiepval in Northern France, where, fifty years before, the 36th (Ulster) Division had written its deeds into history. Some of you were no doubt present also—certainly your President was—and will recall as I do a beautifully warm summer day, with the sun shining on that rolling countryside where so many of Ulster's finest and bravest sons lie to this day.

(*Northern Ireland Area Conference of the British Legion, Belfast, 4th February 1967*)

O'Neill has also been concerned with the organization of his Party, and not least with the calibre of its public representation.

In our system, we have always left the selection of candidates to local Party determination, on the basis that only the active local Party workers know the kind of man or woman most likely to win the seat and represent it well and efficiently in Parliament. Thus we have no centrally approved list of potential candidates, or machinery for the central screening of local decisions.

But local delegates have to take decisions of more than local importance, because in our small House of Commons, every Member matters. No Government can pursue progressive policies unless it has supporters in Parliament willing and able to give effective support for those policies. And it is one of the duties of a governing Party to provide a steady stream of Members who, after appropriate experience, will be fitted to hold junior or senior Ministerial office.

Parliament, and any party which forms a large part of Parliament, ought to reflect a representative cross-section of the best abilities and greatest interests of the country. The great strength of Unionism, after all, in its crucial days of opposition to Home Rule, was the fact that it was a constitutional coalition of so many different elements in Ulster life.

Members ought, of course, to represent their constituents to the best of their abilities. But this does not mean that they should reflect merely the lowest common denominator of the views of their supporters. We want men to whom their constituents will listen, as well as men who will listen to their constituents. We want people who will at all times look at purely local interests against the background of what is good for the country as a whole. Because Northern Ireland is a small place, vested interests tend to be very strong. We need men in Parliament who will listen to their views with the respect due to knowledge and experience, but who will do in the end what they believe to be right.

Above all, Ulster needs today people whose view of politics is a positive one. The recent National Opinion Poll showed many signs of radical movement in local opinion, much of it towards a central position in which reasonable men can stand together. It is that middle ground which is there to be won at the next and subsequent Elections. We need to compromise no single vital principle to win it. But the thinking that to beat an extremist of one colour you must nominate an extremist of another colour is totally misconceived. And I want to make it very clear indeed that in my view there must be a good deal more to being an Official Unionist than merely climbing under the Party umbrella for the purposes of an Election. (*Queen's University Conservative and Unionist Association, 26th January 1968*)

It is, however, the unifying and healing theme which has been predominant in O'Neill's delineation of Unionist principles. Two speeches made in 1968 provide a final illustration of this theme.

Unionism is often so unfairly and inaccurately described by its critics and opponents that those of us who believe in it have the duty, from time to time, to describe it as it is. And the first point to be made is that, unlike a great many political parties, it exists not to divide the community, but to unite it.

I have said it before, and I will say it again: Unionism is more than just a political party, although a political party is its instrument in central and local government. It is a movement, a way of looking at things, a frame of reference which can bring together people from very different backgrounds, many of whom have no formal connection with the party as such.

Unionism has been called sectarian. But I ask those who attach that stigma to us to consider the Manifesto on which we fought the last General Election, and to decide whether there is a single proposition in that policy statement offensive to any religious denomination.

Our policy, as stated in that Manifesto—and it remains our policy up to the next General Election—is to work, through the British connection, for greater economic strength and for the creation of an 'opportunity State' in which no one will be held back by his environment from realizing his full potential.

It was stated yet again in the booklet *Ulster Today and To-morrow*, which the Ulster Unionist Council published very recently. May I read you a few words from it? After setting out all that we propose to do to improve Northern Ireland in a physical sense—through houses and factories, hospitals and roads—the booklet says:

But there is another dimension of a community's life— the quality of its living. Unionism in the years which lie ahead must be concerned with this also. There is no good reason why the unhappy divisions of the past should be perpetuated. Certainly this Ulster of ours will not be as strong, as prosperous and as happy as we would wish until the community is united in essentials.

These are the things that modern Unionism is saying, and people should consider them rather than the words which our enemies try to put into our mouths. I repeat, there is nothing sectarian in the policies of the Unionist Party today, and I welcome the support of anyone who finds in these policies the right and hopeful course for our Province.

Moreover, Unionism sets its face against any division on class or occupational ground. There is no more sad and revealing expression in current use than the one we hear every day about 'both sides of industry', as though the two were drawn against each other in a cup-tie. The expression is symptomatic of strongly-entrenched and very damaging attitudes in Britain, which have had not a little to do with the economic plight in which we now find ourselves.

I would like to see the word 'worker' applied to every man and woman who works, whether for a wage or a salary, whether he wears a white collar or a blue collar or overalls. I refuse to be told that someone like Sir Donald Stokes, chief of Britain's vast new motor empire, and a man who will travel at a moment's notice to Tokyo or Tehran to win export orders, is not as much a 'worker' as the man on his company's assembly lines. Somehow or other we must break down the old, rigid divisions between 'bosses' and employees, and begin to regard all of them as workers with different skills to contribute to the success of the same enterprise.

Someone referred to our country recently as 'Britain Ltd.'. His purpose was to suggest a kind of businessman's Cabinet, and I do not really endorse that idea, because government, like business, has its own professionalism. But the idea of 'Britain Ltd.' or for that matter of 'Northern Ireland Ltd.' is sound in a wider sense: that we are *all* involved in the life of our country, that all of us have something to contribute, that none of us will prosper by leaving it to the other fellow.

It is for reasons such as these that modern Unionism is attached neither to unions nor to employers, but to a concept of the national interest. Increasingly in all the bodies which deal with our economic and industrial affairs—bodies like the Economic Council and Industrial Training Boards—our aim has been to get both 'sides', or as I prefer to put it, both 'parts' of industry sitting around a common table and working together.

Such an approach would be impossible if we were a doctrinaire party. We believe in private enterprise, certainly, because it is private enterprise which has built here the greatest industrial complex in this island. But that belief does not mean we totally reject public enterprise in special cases where this technique has something to contribute. We showed this, for instance, in setting up the Agricultural Trust to explore and develop new growth-points in our agricultural industry. And if nationalization of transport undertakings has not been altogether a happy experience, no one can say we have reached that conclusion without giving the idea a lengthy trial.

Some may say, since Unionism covers such a wide range of interests and—except on the fundamental question of our links with Britain—is far from being dogmatic in its views, that it lacks the purpose and dynamism of a wholly coherent political philosophy. I do not accept that. I never want to see the comfortable and ample garment of Unionism converted into a straightjacket. Nor should we accept that a party system based on sectional or class or economic interests is vital to the health of a nation. Many countries are very well governed by coalitions, and in the United States both great Parties encompass an extremely wide range of views.

As I said at the beginning, Unionism welcomes the support of all, whatever their background or affiliations, who seek through our link with Britain to build a better and more prosperous Ulster. We look always for progress, but we take no narrow view of the way it is to be achieved. We seek not the lowest common denominator but the highest common factor in the life of our community and Province.

(Carrick Unionist Association, 31st January 1968)

You may ask, what do I seek to leave behind me? Chiefly this, to have it accepted by the overwhelming majority of *all* the people of Ulster that only in partnership with Great Britain can we make the progress we all desire. When you think of all that we have achieved over almost half a century, even though a significant section of our population has largely held itself aloof, you realize that there is little we could not do as a united people. Craigavon built the government of Northern Ireland; J. M. Andrews provided the financial foundations for progress; Brookeborough finally secured the constitution. On these foundations, we must build an Ulster fit to match the aspirations of our children.

(N. Tyrone Unionist Association, 24th May 1968)

In 1969 events in the Ulster Unionist Party moved towards a climax. As 'civil rights' agitation continued, the Government decided to establish an impartial Commission—for which the eminent Scottish Judge, Lord Cameron, was later designated as Chairman —to probe the nature and causes of the disturbances which had occurred since October 1968.

This decision prompted the resignation from the Government

*of the Deputy Prime Minister and Minister of Commerce, Mr.
Brian Faulkner. This was followed by the resignation of a second
member of the Cabinet, the Minister of Health and Social Services,
Mr. William Morgan, and by a demand by thirteen Unionist
back-bench Members of Parliament for a change in the Party's
leadership.*

*O'Neill referred to this situation on 28th January in a speech
at Newtownards.*

It must be clear to all today that a struggle is going on for the
heart and mind of our Party. Words like 'leadership' and
'unity' are on the lips of many. The ordinary, loyal Unionist
is puzzled and confused. And so I must speak out, and speak
clearly.

I want you to know, and all the people to understand, that
I have no desire to hang on to the Leadership for its own sake.
I have held the testing office of Prime Minister for six years.
Its burdens are not light ones, nor do they grow less. But it
is my clear duty, with a loyal and united Cabinet behind me,
to continue to fight for these policies we all believe in; policies
which only last month were seen to commend themselves to a
great and influential segment of public opinion; and policies,
too, which will, I believe, sweep the country when next we go
to the Polls. It is also my clear duty—which I will discharge—
to fight for the Constitution of Ulster, and for any measures
needed to protect it against some of the greatest challenges we
have yet faced.

What is good government in Northern Ireland terms today?
It is certainly not abject surrender to every clamour in the
streets. Nor is it stubborn and obstinate resistance to changes
which have got to come, and which are necessary if we are to
secure a happy and united community. No; good government is
provided by an Administration which keeps its head, which
weighs the issues, which formulates its policies wisely and fairly

and is prepared to stick to them. That is good government; that is what my colleagues and I intend to provide.

Tomorrow, as you all know, we will debate in the House of Commons a motion of profound importance. It calls on the House to support the Government in what it is doing to maintain the Constitution; not least by the adoption of prudent and sensible policies which should retain for us the support and sympathy of the British people. When I speak in that debate I will conceal nothing of the basis of my policies for nearly six years. I will lay all my cards on the table; and on that basis I will seek the support of my parliamentary colleagues.

That is how the democratic process ought to work in a free country. There is the place for great issues to be determined— not in the streets, but in Parliament.

And now a word about Party unity. This is something very important to any great Party. With one qualification only, we all must do what we can to secure it. What is that one qualification? It is that Party integrity must never be sacrificed, even in the interests of unity. Just as there are in the world of the Church some people who put unity before principle, so in the world of politics there are those who would put unity before principle. I say that a spurious unity secured by a sacrifice of principle is a snare and a delusion. I do not want people merely to support this great Party of ours; I want them to respect it.

And so, how is unity in the Party to be achieved? Not least, I would suggest, by allowing your leaders to lead, and by cultivating at all levels of the Party a new sense of loyalty and discipline.

Tomorrow's debate in Parliament could be a great healing occasion in our Party. The Motion, calling for support for our Constitution, is one that any Unionist should be proud to support without reservation. And I will speak myself without rancour or recrimination to clear the air. I will place all my policies, all my actions, all my motives, in the context where they belong, support of our Constitution. I hope it will be possible, on the basis of what I say, for Unionists to rally together. For in reality we differ only about means, not about ends. My object is to keep Ulster as an integral and respected part of the United Kingdom. What Unionist could want any other course for our country?

Times of stress and turmoil are often the challenge to greatness. Ours has always been a great Party, but if it can find the right and generous response to present events it can be greater still. In what it says and what it does it can make the Union secure for all time. This is a splendid political opportunity; we must not, and I am sure we will not, miss it.

(*Ards Young Unionist Association, 28th January 1969*)

On Monday, 3rd February, the dissident Unionist Members met as a group at Portadown, and issued a statement attacking the leadership. That evening Captain O'Neill and his colleagues advised the Governor to dissolve Parliament and a General Election was called for 24th February.

The Election which followed was in many ways extraordinary. O'Neill made it clear that he regarded the attacks upon him as being in reality opposition to the moderate policies which he had been pursuing. All of the dissident Members were opposed in their contituencies by unofficial Unionists supporting O'Neill and his policies. The Prime Minister made it clear from the outset that he felt unable to support candidates who had been unwilling to support him; and before the end of the campaign he actively supported some of the 'O'Neillite' unofficial candidates.

The Unionist Manifesto, prepared under O'Neill's direction, made a specific appeal for the ending of the historic religious divisions in the community, and this theme was developed further by the Prime Minister in the course of a televised talk to the electorate.

I want to talk to you tonight about the Election. That means talking to you about your future, for nothing less is at stake.

I have been told that I should not have called this Election at all. I leave it to you to judge. For myself, since it is *your* future which is being decided, I believe that *you* have the right to decide it. I believe that, in a democratic country, when a few people are threatening to push the great majority around, everyone has a right to be heard. Members of Parliament do not always remember that they are the servants, not the masters, of the people as a whole. An Election serves to remind them.

Now, what are you being asked to decide? You are being asked to give us a mandate for all we have been doing to make Ulster a better place to live in. You are being asked to say whether you approve of the motorways, the hospitals, the schools and universities, the houses and factories which make up the New Ulster.

But you are also being asked to take a much bigger decision. It is one which has never been put to you before at any General Election. I am asking you all to trust one another, to accept one another, to respect one another. I am asking you to put our old religious divisions aside to work together for the good of the country.

I think religion ought to be a private matter, a matter of conscience. It has bedevilled Ulster politics for far too long. Let every man worship God in his own way. And let us assume that our fellow-citizens have, for the most part, the same concerns as we do ourselves. They want a steady job. They want a decent home. They want the best for their children. They want, above all, to be allowed to live in peace.

I have been visiting many of you in your homes over the last few days. I looked for that gulf which I am told divides our community and I could not find it. In the homes of the people I found no relish for fighting over old battles once again. You heard a moment ago the words of Edward Carson. I believe his father, who was a firm Unionist but a fair and tolerant man, would have been happy to think that the Prime Minister of Northern Ireland could have received as friendly a welcome as I did in a Roman Catholic house or street or village as in a Protestant area.

In the War I saw a good many men die. They made their sacrifice to overthrow the wicked doctrine that there are superior people and inferior people. I cannot accept any such doctrine here in Ulster—for I am very proud to be British and such ideas are the opposite of everything Britain stands for.

As a Unionist, I believe passionately that Northern Ireland must remain an integral part of the United Kingdom. But that status can never be secure as long as a large section of our population sets its face against it.

I believe that there are few indeed of you who do not appreciate the benefits of the British connection. A farmer does not wish to lose the British agricultural subsidies. A worker at Queen's Island does not want to lose the support which has sustained our shipyard and aircraft factory. And no one really wants to discard the Health Service or lose the benefits of the British Welfare State.

I do not believe that the man or woman who is assured of a fair deal in Northern Ireland will want to sacrifice all the benefits he or she enjoys in the United Kingdom.

I now say this clearly to you all. It is the declared and unmistakable policy of the Unionist Party that *everyone* shall have a fair deal in Ulster. Let there be no more hesitation about supporting the British connection. Its benefits are for all. We recognize no class of citizenship other than the first class.

I ask you all to work together and put an end to strife. Let us repair our damaged reputation in Britain and in the world. Let us show that what a divided Ulster could achieve—which has been remarkable—a united Ulster can surpass.

Many of you over the last three weeks have asked me 'How should I vote on Monday?' You must be guided by your conscience, but you can inform yourself by considering the candidates who seek your vote in the light of these questions.

Can you trust him to preserve the relationship within the United Kingdom which has served us so well, or would he tamper with it and put your future at risk?

Has your candidate been willing over the years to stand up and be counted, or is he rushing at the eleventh hour to show a moderate attitude after years of hard-line activity?

If he is a newcomer to the political scene, do his words and his attitude proclaim his support for fairness and moderation all round?

What does your candidate put first: himself, his Party, or the country as a whole?

My advice to you is this. Look for a candidate whose record for progressive words and deeds is beyond doubt—a man or woman who is trustworthy and consistent. Look for a candidate whose support for the British connection is expressed in a desire to create a community which will be united within and respected without. Bear in mind the well-known words: 'By their works ye shall know them'.

This has been called the Crossroads Election, and indeed it is. We can go forward into a bright future within the United Kingdom as a united people. Or we can sink back into the bog of religious differences. It is with confidence in your common-sense that I place the future of our country in your hands.

(*Party Political Broadcast, 21st February 1969*)

The results of the Election on 24th February were, in the event, somewhat indeterminate. Although two of the group opposed to O'Neill lost their seats to his supporters, in addition to another two who had failed to be re-nominated for the Election by their Constituency Associations, the Prime Minister himself was given a close run in his own constituency by the extreme Protestant leader, Rev. Ian Paisley. Although 'O'Neillism' received about

*twice as much support from the Unionist electorate as 'anti-
O'Neillism', a determined group of dissident Members was again
returned to Stormont.*

*However, at a meeting of the Parliamentary Unionist Party a
few days after the Election, O'Neill's Leadership was confirmed
by a substantial majority, and in the course of his Speech in the
Debate on the Address in the new Parliament, the Prime Minister
made it clear that he would continue along the course he had set
himself.*

Any country needs firm, just and stable government. Events
in Northern Ireland over recent months have illustrated more
than ever the necessity for such a government here. Without
firmness against those who defy the law and disregard the will
of the majority, the conditions for fairness to the community
as a whole cannot exist. On the other hand, firmness without
fairness is mere repression, and the negation of good government. Above all, no consistent line of policy is possible for a
Government which must constantly be looking over its shoul-
der.

The Election was called to seek a mandate for a Government
which will be firm, just and stable. It would be less than frank
of me not to confess that the Election results have, in some respects, been more indeterminate than I had hoped. But those
who are students of politics must pay attention to trends and
directions—and these I think are perfectly clear for all who
are prepared to see them. Candidates committed to moderate
and progressive policies improved their position with the
electorate; others fell back. The wind of change continues to
blow, especially in urban and suburban areas; and in my view
the future rests with those who are prepared to take risks to
unite the country.

No temporary disappointment or partial check will cause
those of us who are committed to policies of reconciliation to

break faith with what has been shown to be the largest single body of opinion in Ulster today.

Our duty now is to act in the spirit of the Declaration of Principles included in our Election Manifesto, and to press on with these specific policies which the electorate have endorsed.

Within the next few days, a Bill to create the office of Parliamentary Commissioner for Administration will be presented to the House. I now wish to inform Honourable Members that, subject to the passage of this Bill into law, it would be our intention to advise His Excellency The Governor to appoint for an initial period as Parliamentary Commissioner for Administration in Northern Ireland Sir Edmund Compton. Sir Edmund is the present holder of the comparable office for the United Kingdom Parliament. He has considerable knowledge of Northern Ireland, since as a senior official in the Treasury some years ago he was concerned with the financial arrangements between Northern Ireland and the United Kingdom.

We have, of course, consulted Her Majesty's Government in the United Kingdom before deciding to recommend this initial appointment, and I am glad to say we have secured their complete agreement to the course which we have proposed. My colleagues and I are convinced that there will be great advantages for Northern Ireland in having obtained the services of a man of such high calibre who has unique experience in this field. It goes without saying, of course, that there will be no fusion of the Northern Ireland and United Kingdom offices. As Parliamentary Commissioner for Northern Ireland, Sir Edmund would act solely on the basis of complaints referred to him by Members of this Parliament.

I am also happy to be able to inform the House of the progress which has been made with the Commission of Inquiry. On the advice of Ministers, His Excellency The Governor has today signed a Warrant appointing Commissioners to 'hold an enquiry into and to report upon the course of events leading to, and the immediate causes and nature of, the violence and civil disturbance in Northern Ireland on and since 5th October 1968; and to assess the composition, conduct and aims of those bodies involved in the current agitation and in any incidents arising out of it'.

As the House already knows, the Commission will be chaired by the distinguished Scottish Judge, Lord Cameron. The membership has been completed by the appointment of two well-qualified Ulstermen. The first of these is Sir John Henry Biggart, Dean of the Faculty of Medicine at Queen's University, and one of Northern Ireland's most eminent and respected sons. The other is Mr. J. J. Campbell, who has not only had a most distinguished career in his chosen field of education, but has given service to many public bodies. Neither of these two men has been active in politics, and I feel sure they can be relied upon to supplement Lord Cameron's legal knowledge and experience with a commonsense appreciation of the local scene. I think it is a good Commission, a strong Commission, and an evidently fair and impartial Commission. And I believe it is the clear duty of every public-minded person, whatever his previous attitude, to co-operate with the Commission now that it has been appointed, so that it may succeed in getting at the truth.

Before I leave this subject, may I reiterate the position of the Government in relation to a Commission of this kind? In the United Kingdom a Royal Commission—of which this is a local equivalent—is a body of the highest standing and importance. A government owes to it every form of assistance and co-operation which it may seek, and when its views on the issues referred to it are made known, a government has an obligation to attach due and proper weight to them. But of course no government can tie its hands in advance to accept any or all of the findings which may or may not emerge. May

I give an example? The Lockwood Committee on Higher Education produced a very comprehensive and well-argued report. The Government considered that report with great care, and to a large extent based its future policies upon it. But we did not accept, for instance, the recommendation that Magee University College should be wound up. We were not prepared, whatever a Committee said, to remove university education from Londonderry. And there are countless other examples from Northern Ireland and the United Kingdom as a whole. A Government must always retain the ultimate responsibility for its decisions. It can and often does seek the best, most impartial and most expert outside advice. But, in the words which President Truman kept in his office 'The buck stops here'.

The Commission will now proceed, and so will all the reforms to which we pledged ourselves in November and again in our Election Manifesto. I have always believed that much of the unrest of recent months has essentially social and economic origins. Above all, poor housing conditions and lack of employment can create a condition of mind in which people lose patience with ordinary democratic remedies. The danger of the situation is that our best and most determined efforts cannot transform the situation overnight. In housing, for example, we have been making and will continue to make the maximum effort to the very limits of our physical and financial resources. I could not help noticing the other day that the Irish Republic, with twice our population, had the same housing target as ourselves, 12,000 a year by 1970. In Irish terms our effort has been phenomenal; and in United Kingdom terms it has kept pace fully with a record effort in Great Britain.

I ask the House, and it is a genuine question not a rhetorical one, to tell us what more could be done. I know full well that the housing need in many areas is enormous, but we cannot do better than our best. As far as allocations are concerned, we are acting to secure evidently fair methods. I see that during the Election campaign the Labour Party in particular attacked the 'Group plus points' system as a basis. It may have its imperfections, but similar schemes have been widely used elsewhere. In any case the idea that some single system can be devised which will be ideal in all situations seems to me an illusion. We are assessing human need, not counting statistical units.

As for employment, we expressed in our Manifesto our determination to work for 'new economic development for all parts of the country'. This we will do, with special emphasis upon the claims of the areas of greatest need, such as Londonderry. What practical alternative has come from the benches opposite to the industrial development and other policies we have formulated? From Socialists of one stamp or another we have heard much about public enterprise. We on these benches are by no means doctrinaire on this issue. At this very moment, the Agricultural Trust is an example of public enterprise in its particular field. But the idea that widespread public enterprise could be some kind of economic cure-all is in my view a delusion. The differences which exist here at the moment, arising out of conditions in the United Kingdom as a whole, would face us whatever the balance between the public and the private sector.

But amidst all the talk of 'civil rights', let me make it clear that we on this side of the House uphold without qualification the civil right of every family to a decent home and of every worker to a decent job. If that right cannot be affirmed in every case, it is not because of any reluctance on our part. The obstacles we face are not political but physical. Housing and employment have been, and will continue to be, in the forefront of our policy. And we will listen with interest and with open minds to every practical suggestion—I repeat, every *practical* suggestion—which comes to us either from this House or from people outside it.

None of these causes, however just, will be advanced in any way by the politics of the streets. In welcoming the Honourable Members for Foyle and Mid Londonderry to this House, may I recall a few words I used here in the House as long ago as 15th October? I pointed to the results of a recent Poll showing that employment and housing were the key issues of public interest, and I went on:

> 'Here are our young people asking us for bread—for the bread of jobs and houses, a decent prosperous life—and are we to offer them instead the stone of discord? . . . The place for political argument is in Parliament, not in the streets. Disorder is the way not to equal rights, but to an equal share of misery and despair.'

I welcome the fact that some of those who organized the politics of the streets have turned to the politics of Parliament. They will not find that we on these benches are deaf to reasonable arguments, reasonably presented. But let it also be clear to those who care nothing for the verdict of the electorate and who are already talking again in terms of coercion and disorder that the vast majority of our people have lost patience with them. They look to the Government to protect their civil right to peace in the streets, and their civil right to have their democratic decisions respected. They will not look in vain. We will give the highest priority to getting the new Public Order Bill on to the Statute Book, so that disorderly demonstrations, provocative counter-demonstrations, private armies and all the undesirable features of recent months can be properly controlled by law. Government and Parliament must be allowed to do their duty without threat and coercion. There is only one Government in this country, and it sits on these benches.

No decent citizen has anything to fear from a fair law, firmly and impartially enforced. This is the foundation of that justice and fairness to which we are totally committed. I re-affirm today our belief in an Ulster in which the obligations and rights of all citizens will be fully recognized; in which religion will be purely a private matter of conscience; and in which all our citizens—seeking the benefits of the British connection and fully sharing in them—will work with equal enthusiasm for the good of the community as a whole. That is the kind of Ulster to which my colleagues and I have dedicated our political careers and for which we will continue to stake our political lives. To give up; to retire from the fray; to say 'enough is enough'; to put compromise before principle—these would be easy and even pleasant courses for some of us to take. I do not imagine that the way ahead for us or indeed for Ulster will be all plain sailing. But my colleagues and I have made promises to the people of Ulster which we feel committed to keep. The stark choice still faces us—Ulster united for prosperity or Ulster divided for disaster. It is a choice, Mr. Speaker, which each one of us must make as this Parliament unfolds. May we have the wisdom, the foresight and above all the courage to make the unity—of aim, if not of methods—in Parliament a model for the wider unity of the country.

(*House of Commons, 4th March 1969*)

CHAPTER 3

Regionalism and Devolution

Northern Ireland, with its own limited powers of parliamentary and executive Government, has a unique position in the United Kingdom, and one which has often led to confusion and mis-understanding. O'Neill has, therefore, been greatly concerned to explain the origins and operation of this system.

The period of his premiership was also one of growing interest in 'regionalism' throughout Britain. The Prime Minister not only acted as an advocate for Northern Ireland's interests in terms of economic development, but he also spoke for all those regions of the nation which, in his view, had not achieved a fair share of prosperity. Nor did he seek to disguise his belief that devolution within the United Kingdom had by no means run its full course, and that some further measure of freedom of action for Scotland and Wales at least was inevitable.

The following speech gives a general outline of O'Neill's views:

It is a curious anomaly that Northern Ireland is a part of the United Kingdom whose position is far better understood, in many respects, outside the United Kingdom than it is in Great Britain. There is, when you think of it, a fairly simple explanation for this. We operate in Northern Ireland within a system of government which is unique in these islands, but fairly common elsewhere in the Commonwealth. It has been my

76

privilege, for example, to know the last two Prime Ministers of the Dominion of Canada, and the Premiers of a number of the Canadian Provinces. They can appreciate—because they have personal experience of it—a two-tier system of government on a federal basis. But the Government of Ireland Act, 1920, which is the basic constitutional statute for Northern Ireland, was a major innovation in the machinery of British government. Others have studied the system. There have been advocates from time to time of separate Parliaments for Scotland and for Wales. But we alone have actually operated a provincial government within the United Kingdom.

To put the matter into historical perspective, it is of course necessary to stress that the Parliament in Belfast did not come about as a result of some overwhelming public clamour for it in the North of Ireland. Our forebears wanted to see the unity of the United Kingdom remain inviolate, and they accepted separate Parliamentary and Governmental institutions as a means of remaining within the United Kingdom.

Yet it is a truism of constitutional development that no man can foresee the impact of a constitutional act. When a party of selfish Barons met at Runnymede for their own limited ends, how could they know that they were underpinning the liberties of England? Who could appreciate that the importation of a German-speaking sovereign would lead to the development of the British Cabinet system where the Prime Minister and not the Queen takes the chair? Or, for that matter, who was to know that the problems of a Labour peer would lead to the emergence of a Conservative Prime Minister?

So it is more important, I would suggest, to consider *how* devolution has operated in Northern Ireland than *why* it originally came into being. And after more than four decades, it is perhaps no bad time to take stock of a significant constitutional development within the British system.

Oddly enough, I would say that the main task of the separate government in Northern Ireland has not been to emphasize differences but to encourage conformity of standards. That is not as straightforward as it sounds. The plain fact of the matter is that the new Parliament and Government of Northern Ireland assumed responsibility for a very under-privileged area of the United Kingdom. Ulster of the Twenties had lower standards of services, of amenities, of wages than almost any part of Great Britain, and so indeed had the whole of Ireland. Moreover the newly-launched ship of state was heading for fearfully stormy waters. In the face of the Great Slump, an area perilously dependent upon a narrowly-based economy saw its unemployment figures rise to astronomical proportions.

Those leaders of Ulster who had devoted their whole energies to ensuring that the people of Northern Ireland remained British citizens were determined that citizenship should be of no second-class variety. Piece by piece, measure by measure, they secured the agreement of successive British governments to a policy of parity. That is to say, Northern Ireland agreed to bear the same burdens as Great Britain, while expecting the same social benefits. What were the implications of this? They were fundamental and far-reaching. Under our constitution we could have decided to levy a lower rate of Income Tax in Northern Ireland than in Great Britain. Cutting our coat according to our more limited cloth, we could have accepted for ever a lower status. Instead, we followed another course. The tax-payer in Belfast pays precisely the same Income Tax as the tax-payer in London. But he also receives the same Family Allowances, the same Old Age Pension, the same Sickness and Unemployment Benefit. If there is a surplus of Northern Ireland revenue after paying for all our services, it goes as a contribution to defence and other Imperial services. If, on the other hand, our revenue is not sufficient to pay for our local services, we receive assistance from Imperial funds.

There are two questions you may ask at this stage. First,

what is the point of having a separate government at all, if your policy is to keep in step with Great Britain? There are several answers to that question. First of all, we must always remember that a Provincial government operates within a National framework. Our constititution does not make us, nor do we wish to be a separate state. We wish to be British in every sense of that word, and we do not think it is tolerable that there should be widely different social service arrangements, for example, in different parts of Britain. Secondly, the policy is not as undramatic as it looks. In a relay-race at the Olympic Games, two runners may breast the tape side-by-side. But that does not mean that they have merely been running monotonously step-by-step. If one runner has been far behind at the baton-change his position at the tape is the result of a great and altogether admirable effort. And we, I can assure you, were very much in the position of that lagging runner in 1920. Thirdly, if we can sustain British standards in Northern Ireland, that is the most we have a right to expect. We are not a wealthy part of this nation, and we cannot expect therefore to offer a higher living standard than in Great Britain but equally, we do not willingly accept less.

The reference to wealth probably provokes a second question in your minds. If we are a relatively poor part of Britain, how do we manage to pay for our services without a subsidy; and if we *are* subsidized, can it be said that our local Government is a viable proposition? That is also a fundamental question. The point here again is the essential unity of Britain. A national society works on the premise that services are made available where they are needed out of the resources of the whole nation. The Regional Plans for Central Scotland and the North-East of England call for the allocation to those areas of capital resources very considerably above the proportion which they might expect on a population basis. Local authorities throughout Britain are enabled to discharge their responsibilities by a system of General Exchequer grants which takes into account both needs and means. In a sense, I suppose it could be said that all the rest of the United Kingdom is subsidized by the wealthy areas of the Midlands and South-East. But it is vain to make this kind of invidious comparison. British citizens everywhere pay the same major taxes and enjoy the same social services. And that is surely right and proper: we cannot have First and Second Divisions in the nation, however admirable they may be in the football league.

I have emphasized this question of parity of status first, because it is of overriding importance. But I do not want you to think that our Government and Parliament merely produce carbon copies of Westminster legislation. In the first place, there are many services which are not simply a matter of paying out cash benefits to the citizen. Let us take housing as an example. Our aim of policy might be described in general as securing for our people housing standards on a par with those prevailing in Great Britain. In practice, this has meant dealing with a formidable backlog, and to do this we have had recourse to various policies which are not applied in England. We have, for example, set up an extremely effective public body, the Northern Ireland Housing Trust, whose record both for production and for quality of accommodation has been most striking.

To put it another way, the fact that we have our own local powers has enabled us to seek *national* ends by *regional* means —that is to say, by means closely attuned to our own particular needs. As an example of this I would cite the provision of employment. I have already mentioned the impact which the Slump had on our narrowly-based economy. Against the background of the 'full employment' policies of successive British governments it has been our aim since the end of World War II to promote diversification of our industry and the creation of new jobs.

Let me state our problems in simple terms. We have the highest rate of natural increase of population in the United Kingdom. We have had to cope with declining employment in such industries as agriculture, linen and shipbuilding because of world trends, greater mechanization, growth of overseas competition and other factors outside our control. As a result of these basic facts, we have normally had a rate of unemployment about four times that of the United Kingdom as a whole. This matter must be kept in perspective. Our post-War unemployment has been much less serious than that of many other countries, and is trivial compared with the pre-War percentages. Nevertheless we live in an age which puts great stress, and very properly so, upon 'the right to work', and it has been our object therefore to take very vigorous measures against unemployment.

We have, therefore, pioneered quite a few methods of promoting industrial investment which are now a commonplace. We maintained an industrial development office in the United States for two years before the United Kingdom Government decided to do so; we initiated years ago a scheme of standard capital grants to industry. We devised types of inducement for new industry which, in terms of generosity and of flexibility, exceeded anything being offered elsewhere in Britain. And added to these and other tangible advantages was the immense intangible advantage of regional government—accessibility of the decision-makers and consequent speed of decision. Red tape tends to be a result of sheer scale. In an immense government machine, the process of consultation and co-ordination can become terribly cumbersome. Within our small administration, I think we have been able to avoid many of these pitfalls. If an individual industrialist has a problem in Northern Ireland, he knows he can come to see me about it. It is not always comfortable to be so accessible—but it is efficient and also, I would suggest, democratic.

How, then, do I see Ulster's future? First of all, and funda-
mentally, I see it as an integral part of Britain—for economic,
for historical, for sentimental and other reasons our ties with
our fellow-citizens are as strong today as they were forty years
ago. I therefore see Ulster developing, not in any sense as an
isolated area, but benefitting from and contributing to the
social and economic progress of the nation. There is a point
in this which we should never forget. The greatness of these
islands was built not upon coal and cotton, but upon brains
and brawn. The material resources which we have enjoyed
are insignificant compared with the reserves elsewhere. It is
from our *human* raw material that we have achieved our present
high standard of living and an honourable place amongst the
nations. Let us not imagine, therefore, that our further advance depends entirely upon automation or technical measures
—vital though these may be. It also depends upon using our
human resources to the fullest extent. In that light, Northern
Ireland, with its reserve of labour, is an under-used national
asset. The heart and core of our policies will be to bring that
asset into fuller use for the benefit both of Northern Ireland
and of the nation.

I am confident that these ends can be achieved through the
flexible and efficient machinery of government which has developed over four decades. Progress in modern times is many-
sided. It is new schools and hospitals; it is the building of
motorways; it is the development of new industries; it is the
building of new towns and the re-development of existing
towns; it is the modernization of agriculture. In all these fields,
we in Ulster have ambitious and forward-looking programmes
to fulfil. As we advance, we will not do so in the spirit of
'Ourselves Alone'. Our economic expansion will help the
United Kingdom towards the achievement of its 4 per cent
growth target. Our Belfast-built ships and aircraft will continue to contribute towards Britain's military preparedness.

Our impressive export record in linen and other goods will help this country towards a more favourable balance of trade. Above all, you can continue to rely on Ulstermen for service to Britain and the Commonwealth. Alexander and Alanbrooke, Montgomery, Templer and Dill—all were men of Ulster stock. It is through men such as these that we have made our mark on British history—and I feel sure that further chapters of this story have yet to be written. Our destinies are linked with yours, and we have confidence that our mutual future will be bright.

(*Royal Commonwealth Society, London,*
12th November 1964)

In any system of devolutionary government, the financial re-
lationships between the central and local Exchequers are, of
course, crucial. Northern Ireland's financial links with Great
Britain are, in practice, rather complex, and O'Neill has taken a
number of opportunities to explain the principles which underlie
them.

I find some people who assume that Northern Ireland as a whole is financed by Great Britain. There is a good deal of use of that very loose word 'subsidy'. And there are those basically hostile to us who try to give the impression that in some way we are not pulling out weight.

Let us, therefore, put the record straight. The £1,000 a year man in Belfast pays exactly the same Income Tax as the £1,000 a year man in Bristol. When he smokes a cigarette or buys a gallon of petrol, he contributes precisely the same amount to the Revenue. In terms of company taxation, Harland and Wolff are no better off than any of their competitors on the Clyde or the Tyne.

To turn to the other side of the ledger, we offer our citizens precisely the same cash social services as their counterparts in

Great Britain. On some of our capital programmes, we are of course spending nowadays at a very high rate per capita; but we are doing so to make up the leeway of earlier times—times when we also paid the same taxes as Great Britain, and handed over a massive Imperial Contribution to boot. Our aim is to secure for our people no more—but certainly no less—than the high standards of living and amenities which British citizens expect.

Let us admit, by all means, that the British agricultural support system has meant an enormous amount to our agriculture. But let us also remember that this is not a dole, but an instrument of national policy designed to keep food prices down. If it is for the benefit of the producer, it is also for the benefit of the consumer—and let us remember that the bulk of Ulster's agricultural produce is consumed in Great Britain. We all know how vital it is, in the national interest, to boost exports and reduce imports. How can anyone say, then, that the maintenance of a productive agriculture in Northern Ireland is not in the national, as well as the local, interest?

Our Budget Expenditure for the current year is estimated at almost £177 million. But the tax revenue of Northern Ireland for the same period is estimated at over £152 million— or more than 85 per cent. Receipts from the United Kingdom Government—other than the payment to us of revenue raised in Northern Ireland—account for only about 6 per cent of the total. What this means, therefore, is that about 94 per cent of our Budget Expenditure is met out of revenue raised from the people of Northern Ireland. Much of it is *collected* by the United Kingdom Government, but it is *our* money which is being collected, and it is ludicrous to lump this in with other sums as if it was a free gift to us.

Some may say—could you pay for all your local services AND pay agricultural subsidies on a local basis AND make a large contribution to defence costs? The answer, of course, is

84

'No'. But it is an answer which virtually every region of Britain except the Midlands and South-East would have to give.

In any case, one cannot assess the contribution which a region makes to the whole nation in purely budgetary terms. The strength of Britain lies not just in the taxation flowing into the Exchequer, but even more in the export orders flowing into industry. And that is where we see that Ulster is playing a very full part. A Skyvan landing on an Alpine airstrip; a Norwegian bulk-carrier on the slipway; Ulster-made optical lenses bound for Germany—these are the signs and tokens of our will to succeed.

(North Belfast Unionist Association,
16th September 1965)

The words 'step-by-step' and 'parity' have become a part of our political vocabulary in Northern Ireland. Unfortunately, those who use them do not always appear to have a real understanding of their meaning.

'Parity' in the widest sense is the overall aim of our policy. I would define it as the position which will be reached when the general level of services and amenities and the general standard of living in Northern Ireland are as high as in Great Britain. This is our long-term goal, which we are trying to attain by every means at our disposal.

'Step-by-step' is one of the means—but only one—which we use in working towards that end. It means that we offer our citizens the cash benefits of the Welfare State at the same level as in Great Britain, and that we seek to attain as high an overall standard in the social services generally. This does *not* mean that in social services—other than the cash social services—we must necessarily adopt the precise policies or financial methods used on the other side of the Irish Sea. We have, for instance, been free to spend twice as much per head on our

85

hospitals, and in housing, to set up an agency—the Housing Trust—which has no English equivalent. We have been free to develop a system of education which we believe to be quite as good as any in the United Kingdom, but which recognizes the existence of special factors here.

Much of our capital expenditure has been not so much a case of 'step-by-step' as of 'step-ahead-of-step'. In those areas where we have leeway to make up, there has been a generous recognition by successive United Kingdom Governments that more than normal measures are needed to close the gap. This has applied, too, in the wider field of economic and industrial development, in which we have maintained since 1945 a more generous and flexible range of inducements than any other part of the country.

There are still other fields where the concepts of 'parity' and 'step-by-step' do not really apply at all—nor should they. In purely social questions I believe that it is right that we should do what *we* think is best, taking full account of course of what is done in Great Britain, but also bearing in mind the particular circumstances of Ulster and—not least—the views of those who return us to Parliament.

There are a good many members of the Opposition who want to have the best of both worlds. On the one hand, they want to be able to denigrate our political institutions by claiming that we are a mere 'rubber stamp' with no real powers. On the other hand, whenever some specific policy adopted in London happens to appeal to them, we are told that 'step-by-step' demands that we should follow suit.

This is an age of 'regionalism', and it is a pretty fair bet that within Great Britain we will see further measures of decentralization on the executive, if not on the legislative, level. This whole process will be pointless, however, unless regional government is properly responsive to the special needs, the special traditions and, not least, the special views of its own area.

86

I hope, therefore, that no one who hears about 'step-by-step' will see the Parliament of Northern Ireland as a kind of pet dog trotting at its master's heels. 'Parity', in the widest sense, is the end; 'step-by-step' is a part of the means; but in many fields we have the right and indeed the duty to go our own way.

'Step-by-step' assures Northern Ireland citizens of the same pensions when they retire, the same benefits if they are unemployed, as are received by the people of Great Britain. Under our new legislation recently introduced at Stormont they will also be assured of substantial help to tide them over any period of redundancy. In any society, there are always some industries which are contracting while others are expanding. This means that many people will have to contemplate a change of employment, and I think it is only right that society should provide a cushion against the hardship which can result from that process.

But we should also consider some of the benefits which we in Northern Ireland enjoy which are outside the scope of 'step-by-step' but are rather the results of the forward-looking policies of our own Government. In housing, I have already mentioned the position of the Housing Trust, but in addition we have had special measures in Northern Ireland to encourage the owner-occupier, which have no counterpart elsewhere. I like to think that, just as the old Land Purchase Acts encouraged the farmer to take over the ownership of his land, so our housing policy has encouraged home-ownership. More than other parts of the United Kingdom, we have demonstrated our belief in 'the property-owning democracy'.

In the attraction of industry, it is only very recently that anything similar to our Capital Grants scheme has been introduced in Great Britain, and the grant rates there are substantially lower. There is, understandably, a great deal of interest in *new* industry, but no one should overlook what has been done to modernize the older industries of the Province which still employ so many of our people. It is in no small degree due to these policies that such industries as linen and shipbuilding have made a massive and impressive come-back from some of their earlier difficulties. In 1960 the British Government set up an office in New York to attract new American industries to this country. But it was not first in the field; the Northern Ireland Government already had an officer there three years before the British office was set up.

What all this means is that we need, more than ever, the ideas and hard work of this community. Our connection with Great Britain gives us the firmest of foundations, but it does not exempt us from the need to build ourselves. With our own Parliament and our own Government machine, we have built-in advantages over any region of Britain. We are close to the needs and desires of our own people, and can seek within Northern Ireland suitable Ulster solutions to the problems which face Britain today.

(*Court Ward Unionist Association, Belfast,
18th October 1965*)

O'Neill has always felt very strongly about the economic and social imbalance between London, the South-East and the Midlands on the one hand, and most of the rest of Britain on the other. Whenever afforded a suitable platform in London, he has used it to encourage a positive attitude at the centre towards these regional problems. The speech which follows is typical of his message on these occasions:

I come from a part of the United Kingdom whose attachment to the City of London goes far beyond mere sentiment. In that settlement of Ulster which made our Province what it is today, the City played a vital and an honourable part. Our own second city bears the proud name of *London*derry, and maintains with pride its ancient connections with the Honourable the Irish Society. I can speak, too, from a family point of view, since my family sat at Westminster as representatives from County Antrim for a continuous period of almost a hundred years.

The relationship of this great metropolis with the rest of our nation is, however, one of the most difficult problems which Britain faces in the second half of the Twentieth Century. It was Benjamin Disraeli who wrote strikingly of the 'two nations' in our society. He had in mind at that time the appalling disparity between man and man; the anomaly of riches and poverty cheek by jowl with each other; the inequality between those who inherited the earth without effort and those who did not even have the opportunity of making an effort.

Much of the history of modern times records the struggle of this and other nations to right these wrongs. Success here and elsewhere has been incomplete, but it is now a matter of means rather than ends. We may not achieve affluence for all; but we can and should abolish poverty in our time. In our satisfaction with this progress, we can too readily come to believe that the fundamental problems of our society are on the way to solution.

I would like to bring you from Northern Ireland the thought that there are other tasks, most difficult yet most rewarding, to which we must now set our hands. We have dealt with the most obvious and most unjustifiable of personal inequalities. We have only begun to cope with the vast problem of regional inequalities.

One of the features of Britain which most impresses the overseas visitor is its vast variety. Arriving here with a preconceived notion of London alone as a sort of perpetual Baker Street shrouded in fog, he is stunned to discover the tremendous range of landscape, accents and behaviour patterns which Britain can show. Much of our greatness as a nation stems from that diversity. The Scots have sent many occupants to 10 Downing Street, while we in Ulster have chiefly concentrated upon the mass-production of Field-Marshals: Montgomery and Alexander, Alanbrooke, Templer and Dill. We have long taken this abundance, this regional vigour somewhat for granted.

I want to tell you tonight that the most imaginative and bold measures are needed if the balance of this nation is not to be greviously and disastrously upset. I am sure that you Londoners have been reading your Buchanan Report and thinking carefully about its implications. You must be asking yourselves how this great accumulation of population can—except at a cost almost too astronomical to contemplate—stave off its ultimate strangulation by traffic. You must often ask yourselves, too, whether the inflation of property values and the pressure upon services in this area can go on for ever.

All over Britain, at places some hundreds of miles from this Guildhall, great numbers of your fellow-countrymen are asking themselves different questions. The school-leaver in Newcastle-upon-Tyne is wondering how on earth he will ever find an apprenticeship. The civil engineer about to graduate from a Scottish university is wondering whether to drift South into England for a job, or whether to look for a position further afield. The promising scientist from Belfast is asking himself how he will adapt to life in Southern California.

It is an absurd and tragic situation. Here we are, over fifty million people on these tiny, rather isolated islands, poor in raw materials, competing with each other for the meagre land available, balancing our precarious prosperity upon the knife-edge of international trade. Yet, in the midst of this situation we continue as a nation to waste much of our finest asset, the human resources whose qualities of character and intellect have, against all the probabilities elevated us to a high rank amongst the powers of the world.

Even in Scotland, in North-East England and in Northern Ireland most of our people enjoy an unprecedented prosperity. The days of the Thirties, of truly massive unemployment and distress, have gone, I trust, for ever. We should not think of the problem in these melodramatic terms. But in Northern Ireland today nearly 7 out of every 100 insured employees are looking for a job, and in other areas of Britain remote from London the position is comparable, though less serious.

I am speaking about this tonight not because we expect charity or want sympathy. Far from it—we are a proud people, accustomed to standing firmly upon our own feet. I am speaking about it because our position in Northern Ireland affects the position of everyone who is here tonight. I base that statement not upon some philosophical idea of the unity of man, but upon hard economic facts.

We have suddenly become aware as a nation—and I think we can thank NEDDY for this—that the tasks we face demand of us some real prescience and planning, some sense of national aims and purposes. We have the difficult but stimulating competition of the Common Market to face. We have before us the prospect of colossal expenditures for higher education, for a technological revolution within industry, for a vast increase in research and development. How on earth are we to bear these burdens without becoming uncompetitive in the market-place of the world?

There is only one answer. We must achieve a more rapid rate of economic growth. Since this is the case, we can see the situation in Northern Ireland and other under-employed areas as something more profound than a social injustice. It is a monstrous and stupid economic waste. If we are to achieve a faster rate of economic growth, we must bring more of the under-used resources of these areas into use. And when I say WE, I mean this whole nation.

Less than two weeks ago, I had my first meeting with Sir

Alec Douglas-Home, and we discussed some of these problems. I was left with the impression that he attaches the greatest possible significance to the question of regional development, and that it will have a foremost place in the thinking and planning of the Government. I was immensely encouraged by that fact.

Of course, all this talk of regional development does not make sense if its simply a question of bolstering-up dreary places which can never, by any stretch of imagination, be economic. But Northern Ireland—to take it merely as an example—is by no means that sort of place. We man the shipyards which built the *Canberra*, Britain's largest post-War passenger liner; our aircraft factory pioneered vertical take-off technique in this country; the great American chemical combine of Du Pont chose our area for its first plant in Europe; our traditional linen industry is a leading dollar-earner for Britain; yet alongside it has developed Britain's most concentrated complex of artificial fibre production. We have seen more than 170 new industrial enterprises grow up in our midst since World War II. In every feature of our life we have worked to meet the needs of a modern industrial society. We have the land, the people, the electric power, the roads, the housing to carry a still more dramatic expansion of our economy.

In a very real sense, Britain needs the success of Northern Ireland, of Central Scotland, of the North-East of England to achieve its own essential rate of progress. Without us, you will be like a car trying to win a Grand Prix with a missing cylinder. And for you in Greater London the stakes are greater still. Unless the periphery's attractions can be made more clear, the centre will continue to grow. Like a magnet, London and the South-East will draw into itself more and more of Britain's people and its resources. That would be a disaster for the nation, which it would weaken, and a tragedy for London, which it would asphyxiate. A writer coined for this development the term MEGALOPOLIS. It is neither in your interest nor in ours that such trends should be allowed to continue.

You may ask: what can we in London do about this situation? May I make some suggestions to you? You should not merely accept but welcome and even demand measures to limit the growth of this congested area. You should endorse and support a tough policy towards industrial expansion here. You should judge with sympathy and vision the financial and other needs of Northern Ireland and other distant areas of your country. A degree of redistribution of *personal* income has long been accepted as fair; we will come to accept, I believe, that a degree of redistribution of *regional* income is also fair.

But above all, it is important that the pride which Londoners feel in their metropolis should not prejudice their judgment of other areas. You may find it difficult to believe this, but the real stumbling-block in the way of a firm locating a major expansion in an area such as ours may not be a serious economic objection, but the reluctance of key people and their wives to consider transplanting their lives. Too many still believe that somewhere north of Oxford there lies a dark, inhospitable, unfamiliar country, whereas the people across that little strip of water are utterly foreign and remote.

The sad thing is that these prejudices are, for the most part, unfounded. Those who talk vaguely of the delights of the London theatres, may well see only one show a year. They choose to commute an hour and a half each day in each direction to an absurdly expensive house. They see the countryside at weekends in the midst of a queue of traffic. Yet they are convinced that theirs is the best, indeed the only possible way of life in Britain.

May I end on a note of example? A company had its factory in the London area. Demand for its products was growing, yet it was difficult to maintain even the existing work force in

93

an area where competition for labour was keen. In spite of this, the company wanted to add a major extension at its London plant. The Board of Trade said 'No. We will not give you an Industrial Development Certificate. You must look elsewhere'. So they looked at the development areas of Great Britain, and eventually at Northern Ireland. And we made them this offer. 'We will build a factory for you and let it to you at 1s. 6d. a square foot a year. We will pay a third of the cost of your machinery and equipment. We will pay a large slice of the cost of training your operatives.' They considered this offer, they took into account the plentiful supply of labour, and they decided that economic commonsense pointed to Ulster.

But when the time came to appoint a manager, he was unhappy, and—perhaps more important—his wife was unhappy. They left London with gloom, convinced that they would be miserable. But what happened? They were able to buy a far better house than they could afford in London. Instead of sweating for an hour and a half to get to the factory on the train, it takes ten minutes by car. They motor on uncluttered roads. They belong to a golf club and a sailing club at rates which even before the War would have been considered unbelievable in London. And you would have to drag them back to London in chains.

What I have been trying to say tonight is that we in Britain need each other. Ours is a small country, depending for its success upon human qualities. As long as those human qualities are wasted, we will not have realized our full potential as a nation. This, I believe, is the greatest problem and the greatest opportunity facing us today.

(*Guild of Freemen of the City of London,*
4th December 1963)

Increasingly, O'Neill has considered inevitable some further move-ment towards devolution in other parts of the United Kingdom.

94

I believe that when the history of these times comes to be written, one of its significant themes will be the reversal of what I might call the 'metropolitan trend'. It may seem a paradox that the age of wider groupings of nations has also been the age of new concern about regions within the nation. Yet we can all discern this problem at the human level. How do we operate the huge, modern school or the vast, impersonal business organization and still preserve the value and distinctiveness of the individual?

I hold to the belief that diversity is a very important part of 'the wealth of nations'. I do not want to see the United Kingdom, whether as an element of a greater Europe or not, become a kind of standardized and bland subtopia. And because these are my beliefs I welcome very much the growing awareness in this country over the last ten years of the problems and opportunities of regionalism.

There is a moral issue here as well as an economic one. We have long ago concluded in this country that, when an individual has worked hard for many years, he has a right to something better in his retirement than the scrap-heap of poverty. Yet there are whole regions of Britain which in past generations have contributed a very great part of the wealth of this country, but which have at times seemed to be facing no brighter a future than the contemplation of the debris of their better days. I do not suggest that the answer is to prop up declining industries for ever, or to try to stimulate new growth in every derelict mining village. But I do hold the view that it is wrong to allow any great historic region of this country, with human potential waiting to be tapped, to choose between emigration and unemployment.

Happily our Governments, Conservative and Labour, have shown a growing concern with this matter. By financial and fiscal measures, by control of the location of industry, by redirection of capital investment, new hope has been brought to many places.

The most recent development has been the move towards some limited degree of regional autonomy. Scotland, of course, has its own Departments, and so to a lesser extent has Wales. But for the first time the English Regions, through their advisory Economic Councils, have been given a genuine local voice in their development. This may well prove to be merely an intermediate step. Almost certainly the Royal Commission which is now examining English local government will recommend some form of much wider local government area. In this or in some other way, I look to see eventually some kind of elected government body responsible for development of the region.

(National Conference of Royal Institute of Chartered Surveyors, Belfast, 28th June 1967)

In our devolutionary set-up, progress can only be made if both Governments co-operate and achieve a cordial understanding. This is made easier in the present case by the British Government's emphasis on regional matters. To secure balance in the nation, to breathe fresh air into the regions and prevent strangulation of the metropolis—these are policies which can be endorsed by Ulster and Wales alike.

I must say that I myself believe it inevitable that devolution within the United Kingdom has not run its full course. The establishment of regional planning boards and councils is a first stage, and no doubt the reassessment of local government will result in some form of wider groupings. In the long run, I believe that it will be in the interests both of Westminster and of the regions themselves to set up some kind of elective body to which the local planners and executive can be responsible. When this occurs, I also believe that the Northern Ireland experience will be of real interest and value. We have found that our own local institutions of government have given us a flexibility and a responsiveness to local conditions which we would not otherwise enjoy.

Let me hasten to say that I do *not* endorse local 'nationalism'. As the nations form wider political and economic groupings, I believe a narrow separatist approach becomes increasingly inappropriate. I approve of a measure of regional devolution not as a step to weaken the nation, but as a step to strengthen it. It would allow the great assembly of the whole nation to devote more of its time to the weighty issues which confront Britain in a European and international setting.

I look forward to the day when we will be strengthened as individuals by a chain of loyalties which supplement each other: to our family, to the local area, to our Region or Principality, to the nation, and to some wider scheme of things in which Britain will play a notable part. This may seem visionary, but the visions of today are blueprints for the realities of tomorrow.

(*Luncheon for Secretary of State for Wales, 3rd July 1967*)

CHAPTER 4

Physical and Economic Planning: A Time of Change

The O'Neill premiership has seen a significant movement towards a better planned and co-ordinated development of the economy, and upon the infrastructure of physical services on which it rests. Two reports by internationally known experts have established the principal aims of policy. That of Sir Robert Matthew on the Belfast Region, which called for a limitation of the physical growth of Belfast and the establishment of growth points (notably the new city of Craigavon) elsewhere, was supplemented and extended by the report of Professor Thomas Wilson on the economy, which recommended new lines of economic strategy for the period 1964–70. Equally notable was the report of a Committee on Higher Education, chaired by Sir John Lockwood, which led (inter alia) to the foundation of a New University of Ulster at Coleraine.

An early achievement of the new administration was the removal of an impasse to the recognition by government of the central body of the trade union movement, the Northern Ireland Committee of the Irish Congress of Trades Unions. This opened the way to trade union participation in an advisory Economic Council, and to full union co-operation in the very extensive programme of labour training which now got under way, and soon developed impressive momentum.

PHYSICAL AND ECONOMIC PLANNING

To cope with the new challenges of economic and physical development, O'Neill carried out a radical re-organization of the machinery of government, notably by setting up new Ministries of Development (of the physical infrastructure) and of Health and Social Services.

The new programmes had an encouraging impact upon the major economic indicators, including unemployment. Unfortunately, by the second half of 1966, the economic downturn in Britain as a whole inevitably led to a deceleration in the rate of new development.

In a period of rapid change, various tensions have developed. O'Neill has sought many times to demonstrate why change is necessary, and to illustrate his sympathy with the human problems which it creates.

Addressing a World Economic Conference organized in Belfast by the Junior Chamber of Commerce, O'Neill referred to the theme of the human implications of planning.

Let us never forget the basic human factor in our plans. Economic planning, with its emphasis on priorities, presents many individuals and groups with the need for change. Agricultural economies become industrialized; the form of the industrial structure itself must be adapted to new circumstances; and individual men and women may find their environment or their skills overtaken by events which they do not clearly understand.

Our task is not, therefore, merely to plan; it is to convince people of the need for planning and of the benefits which it can bring. All economic history shows clearly how people will strike out blindly against forces which they do not understand. The men who wrecked the early machinery of the Industrial Revolution have their counterpart in every age. In retrospect, they have all the futility of those who struggle against the inevitable. Yet we owe them, in our own time, sympathy and understanding. It is always better to explain than to enforce.

Somehow or other we have to convert economic jargon into terms which the ordinary citizen can understand. This is not merely because democratic governments need the support of an electorate. It is also because traditional attitudes, if we do nothing to change them, can be an enormous obstacle to economic progress.

(*Belfast, 9th April 1965*)

We want to build the Opportunity State, in which no man will be imprisoned by his environment, and in which every citizen will have the chance to realize his full potential. I have seen some criticism of late on the theme that the Government has not fully succeeded in putting across to the mass of people the reasons for its plans. There may be some justification for this, in that terms like 'infrastructure' and 'linear development' mean much to the expert, but little to the man in the street. But if the methods and the terminology are complex, the aims are quite simple. We want to marry housing development and industrial development so that we no longer have the absurd situation that, in an area of high unemployment, firms are frantically searching for the workpeople they need. We want to acknowledge the arrival of the motor-car age, by providing the modern roads which will give rapid access to all parts of Northern Ireland. We want to prevent, before it is too late, the traffic strangulation of our towns and cities. We want to preserve the countryside while it is still fair and green, so that succeeding generations will not curse us for our neglect and our lack of concern. These are not politicians' visions or planners' dreams: they are the vital needs of a Province which can achieve a dramatic break-through in conditions of life.

And the other key word is 'partnership'. The Government is not, and has no wish to be, a kind of executive steamroller, .

flattening everything in its path. This country cannot achieve the higher standards which are possible without the co-operation of local authorities, of the business community, of management and the trade unions. When Ulstermen are truly united, they are a formidable force—as the history of this century has shown on more than one occasion. But too often we dissipate our energies in argument about comparative trivialities.

(Belfast, 22nd May 1965)

Above all, O'Neill has emphasized the need for human concern, both to explain the need for planned development and to temper its effects.

It is a truism that we live in an age of change. It may be asked: has not the entire history of man's life on earth been a story of change and development? To a degree that may be true, but the evolution of men, institutions and ideas has for the most part been an extremely gradual process. The challenge of this age is the enormous change of pace. World population, whose growth over many centuries was almost imperceptible, is now the object of a threatening multiplier effect. The art of destruction, subject for centuries to refinements only of degree, has changed its entire nature and dimension. Within a century and a half we have gone from the maximum speed of a galloping horse to the revolutions of satellites which girdle the whole earth. No part of the world has escaped the implications of such changes. Danger and opportunity have both been heightened; mankind has to adjust to living dangerously.

When we shift our gaze from the wider world picture to a small, rather closely-knit community like Northern Ireland, we see some special aspects and problems. Our population has typically had very deep roots in various loyalties and affiliations—geographical, occupational, religious and so on. This was in some ways a place of very fixed sympathies, and whatever the shortcomings of that situation, people knew where they stood. Suddenly many of the old positions seem to be shifting; familiar landmarks cannot be so clearly seen; and people have to adjust to new factors and new forces in their lives. Let us take as an example the forces of physical change and development. A farmer occupies land which his ancestors have cultivated, perhaps for generations. Out of the blue, because of a new town or new motorway or new factory, that land has to be vested. One of those situations then arises in which the interests of the individual have to be weighed against those of the community as a whole. Sometimes, but not always, there is room for compromise. At other times the wider public interest has to prevail—but one of the principal concerns of government and of all public authorities must be to ease hardship in such situations, and if we can, to explain adequately the nature of the particular public interest, which is not always as self-evident as experts may believe.

Change and how to handle it is one of the issues which public men and public authorities ought to be thinking about. The other is the sheer complexity of the issues in which the individual becomes involved. Democracy—let us face the fact —is better attuned to broad simple issues than to complex and highly technical decisions. The democratic process is more accustomed to saying 'We are attacked; we must defend ourselves' than to weighing the effects and implications of a tariff agreement or a monetary crisis or a plan for capital investment.

We have to face the fact that many of the activities of the public sector have become almost incomprehensible to the community in whose interest they are being carried on. The implications of this fact can be profoundly disturbing. It accounts for much of the detachment, the 'couldn't care less' approach, the revolt of the young against the organization of society, which we see here and everywhere also. Alienation of government from the governed, of town from country, of employer from workpeople—these are some of the chief ills of our age.

(*Community Work Conference, Magee University College, Londonderry, 5th June 1968*)

O'Neill has continually pointed out that, in terms of economic development in general and new industrial development in particular, only international standards are relevant. He has, too, sought to draw lessons from the experience of other countries.

Although Britain was the first country in the world to develop an industrialized economy, many countries are now more productive and more efficient. We built in Britain a great industrial fabric of iron and steam, coal and textiles. Even here in Ulster, on the fringes of the British Industrial Revolution, we were very early in the field in many industries. We were talking textiles in Ulster centuries before Hong Kong became a British colony. Our ships were sailing the oceans of the world before Japan had begun to emerge as a significant industrial power. Yet, with all this wealth of experience, it takes more men to produce a ton of steel or build a house than it does in the countries of some of our competitors, and notably the United States.

My second starting-point is that, in spite of all the talk about the 'technological gap', the people of these islands have a considerable innovative genius. No one would be interested in draining our brains if they were not good and lively brains. Ever since the Industrial Revolution began, and right up to today, many of the most significant ideas in science and technology have originated in Britain. But we have often been slow to cherish and support our innovators. Barnes Wallis was appreciated more readily elsewhere. According to one count, of 100 major advances in basic industrial technology in the years since 1945, Western Europe accounted for nearly half, as against some 30 per cent for the United States. And in Western Europe, Britain has the most advanced technological structure.

Yet, in spite of our 'lead time' in experience and our innovative genius, our competitive position has been poor. What is the reason? High wage costs in relation to competitors? I doubt it. The United States, in spite of its high overall deficit, has a large surplus on its balance of visible trade, although it pays the highest wages in the world. A degree of geographical remoteness? Certainly our position is no worse than that of Japan. High cost or erosion of supplies of basic raw materials? But many of the vast profitable modern industries depend upon brains, not bulk.

I think that two changes in particular must be made. First, we must achieve a substantially more efficient use of labour. To say this, in an area which needs to create more jobs rather than the reverse, may seem a paradox. But we have always recognized, when assisting and encouraging Ulster industry to modernize, that one outcome might be a reduction in some labour forces. We cannot evade the inescapable logic of the market-place. I always think of the illustrations which the life insurance companies use to demonstrate the adverse effects of over-weight. (It is, perhaps, as well that I should introduce this subject when we have already eaten.) They tell us that an overweight man is carrying the equivalent of a heavy suitcase with him everywhere. Many aspects of British industry are, I fear, still carrying too much fat compared with their competitors. Now I do not pretend that dieting, individual or corporate, is an easy process. But we cannot as a nation afford the attitude of 'Eat, drink and be merry . . .'.

The second really important change we need is to secure somehow or other a more rapid and effective commercial exploitation of scientific and technical innovation. This is something which the United States does outstandingly well. The very high cost of labour has made industry there peculiarly receptive to the introduction of devices which save labour—from the sewing-machine to the computer. The size and wealth of the domestic market has encouraged mass-production, and the defence and space programmes have had important side-effects.

But, above all, surely it is in management techniques and skills that Americans have stood out? In the organization of business and decision-taking; in the development of specific management skills; in the status of institutions like the Harvard Business School, there are lessons for us to learn.

I can think of no greater necessity for Ulster and for Britain than for thoroughly competent and professional management. This already exists in the best concerns here and in other parts of the United Kingdom, and in this context may I say how very proud we are that it was an Ulsterman from Lisnaskea who spear-headed Rolls-Royce's export triumph in the United States? This bears out what I have been saying about the British genius for technical innovation, and shows what rich rewards can be won where it is backed up by managerial drive of the highest quality. But a performance like this shows Britain at its best, and it remains true that there is substantial room for improvement in overall standards. We are extremely conscious of this problem within the Government itself. Today much of our work is not administrative and parliamentary in the old sense, but managerial. We have had to develop sophisticated management services, including computerization. We are adapting all the time to new methods and new techniques. On matters of this kind I think a continuous exchange of ideas —and perhaps to some extent even of personnel—between government and industry would be useful.

(*British Institute of Management, Belfast, 29th April 1968*)

A principal social aim of economic policy has, of course, been a reduction in unemployment.

The provision of jobs, schools and houses is a social issue; in a time of expansion it is an economic issue; but it is also at all times a moral issue. Prolonged unemployment can be a cancer eating away a man's self-respect and human dignity. At one level it has to be approached coolly and dispassionately, with the expertise of the economist or the statistician. But at another level it must be confronted with that profound indignation which underlies every sustained movement for social or economic reform.

It must be said, however, that this question of providing jobs for the people imposes obligations upon the individual as well as upon the community. In general we must applaud the fact that the Welfare State, as we know it in this country, protects the individual in many cases against undue hardships. Unfortunately it can also provide a cushion for a minority of malingerers who do not exactly seek employment with enthusiasm. In some parts of our Province today there are firms which would like nothing better than to expand their labour force. They are unable in many cases to do so partly because adequately qualified people are not available, but partly too because people are not always flexible enough to be willing to adapt themselves to new circumstances.

It is not always sufficiently understood that we cannot provide for every unemployed person in Ulster a job at his present location and in his present trade. If this were possible, it would be much simpler for those of us who have to deal with this difficult problem. Unfortunately what we have to meet are not the needs of the various areas of Northern Ireland or the needs of the Government but the needs of industry itself. New firms do not come to Ulster with the idea of doing us a favour. We can employ our whole armoury of inducements and persuasion to influence their decision, but in the last resort the decision is theirs.

We have found from many years of experience that some

types of industry will locate only at fairly large centres of population. This is why part of our industrial strategy for the future involves the building-up of a number of key 'growth points' throughout the Province. In a sense it could be said that, over the past few years our industrial development programme has entered a new phase. Whereas it used to be a problem to interest any substantial body of new industry in Ulster, today it is rather a question of trying to meet the needs of a very large volume of interested companies. The emphasis nowadays must be placed upon such things as labour and management training; the improvement of communications; the provision of housing and vital services; and upon a many-sided modernization of the local environment.

(Coleraine, 12th May 1966)

O'Neill has paid frequent tribute to the co-operative attitude of the Ulster unions.

What a tragedy it would be if our successors were to say that this age, in which a uniting Europe moved on to a new level of industrial and economic performance, was also the age in which our own country abdicated its position as a world economic power, and sought the haven of a safe mediocrity!

I am sufficient of an optimist to believe this will not happen. But if the danger is to be averted, employers, unions and the Government really must become an effective Triple Alliance in the national interest. This does *not* mean that we could, or should expect any of these groups to ignore its own basic interests. The profit motive may seem wicked to some people; but the loss motive is the royal road to bankruptcy. Unions must continue to be concerned with the conditions of employment of their members. Surely what is needed above all else, however, is a realization that the best interests of any group are not necessarily only its short-term interests. It would be a pity if we were to be so preoccupied with dividing the existing national cake that we allowed the oven to go out.

In this job I have had the chance of meeting a good many of the leading trade unionists here in Ulster. I have been greatly heartened and encouraged to find how many of them do in fact think in this long-term dimension. Northern Ireland has been, in recent years, an industrial economy undergoing a process of very rapid change. Completely new industries, once totally unknown to us, have been springing up. We have had to cope not only with new products and technologies but with the different approaches to business of great American and Continental concerns. It is no secret that most of those who are planning big new enterprises here have discussions with union representatives at a very early stage. If these men were restrictive, or narrow-minded, or unwelcoming they could very easily lose for us some of these promising new developments. But this is not the case. Far from it; the incoming industrialist finds he is talking to men who want to see industry grow and prosper quite as much as he does. And this is terribly important.

I would commend also the approach of leading trade unionists to the vital question of labour training. Here is something quite crucial in a pattern of industrial change. We simply must have a manpower policy which can cope with the needs, not of an old Ulster which is passing from the scene, but of the new Ulster which is emerging.

(*A.T.G.W.U. Conference, Newry, 18th August 1966*)

O'Neill has spoken often of industrial development; but, of course, a principal pillar of the local economy remains its agriculture. The Prime Minister has given his view of its position and prospects.

The well-being of our agriculture depends mainly on two factors. The first of these is our connection with the United

Kingdom from which we benefit by unimpeded access to the British market and by inclusion in the United Kingdom agricultural support system. The second major factor in our drive to increase the prosperity of Ulster's farming community is the technical skill and business sense of our farmers. Because we are an integral part of the United Kingdom, British conditions of production and marketing are assured for us, but the second factor, the skill of our farmers, is something which we must look after ourselves. If we are to ensure a full rich future for our farmers, both collectively and individually, we must continually be trying to improve the quality of our produce and reduce our costs of production.

Farming is now a highly-skilled business. One has only to look at the curriculum for the one-year course here at Greenmount to have this fact hammered home. This course, designed, I would emphasize, for boys who are going to become practising farmers, includes such topics as mechanics, chemistry, zoology and botany. I think this illustrates very clearly the changing nature of the farmer's job. There was a time not so long ago when a skilled farmer needed to know no more than that certain results followed certain actions. This kind of knowledge, based on experience and observation, while still valuable, is no longer enough. Today's farmer must know more about *why* and *how* these results and actions are interrelated.

Because of his increasing skills today's farmer can command financial returns sufficient to reward the highest levels of intelligence and education. The time has gone when the bright boys were sent out from the family farm to find places in industry and the professions while the plodder remained at home to take over the farm. Now farming provides both intellectual challenge and financial incentive to the brightest boy in the family—and even he needs the best possible education. This education should, if possible, include a good general grounding, particularly in such subjects as English, Mathematics and Science, followed by at least a one-year course at a College like Greenmount.

The Minister of Agriculture has said that he hopes the Government will be able to provide sufficient college places to enable every young farmer to enrol for a one-year course as well as to allow a smaller number to do an advance course. I am, of course, entirely with him on this. The time must come —and come fairly quickly—when the farmer who is *not* college-trained will be the exception.

Like all industries, agriculture must become more productive if rhe standard of living is to continue to rise. Unfortunately, the market for food in Britain, as in other countries, is unlikely to grow significantly faster than the population. Very determined efforts are being made—and I applaud them—to sell Ulster's agricultural products on world markets. In seed potatoes, for example, we have already achieved something of an international reputation, and our carefully-guarded freedom from many plant and animal diseases is an enormous asset. It would, however, be less than realistic to expect that we can ever hope to sell more than a marginal proportion of our agricultural output outside the British market.

It follows from this that the movement of workers out of agriculture is likely to continue for some time. On the one hand, this means that the Government must press ahead vigorously with plans to encourage alternative employment. You can see the results of that policy in the myriad of new firms now prospering in the Province. Happily, some of the most significant of recent developments have been directly based upon our agricultural production.

But if agriculture can expect to employ fewer people in the future, no one should make the mistake of considering it a declining industry. It will continue to be one of the main props of our economy. It will operate in a highly competitive world, where the emphasis will be on raising productivity and pruning costs. It will be an industry in which the new generation of scientific farmers—the generation represented here to-day—should be able to expect a rising standard of living.

To the students, I would say this: Yours will be the privilege of witnessing yet another stage in the evolution of the oldest industry known to mankind. You will face, as all your predecessors have done down the ages, the vagaries of soil and climate, the threat of the wet season or the inroads of pest or disease. But you will face them with the new weapons which knowledge and research have given you. All of us here and throughout Ulster wish you well; the future is in your hands.

(*Agricultural College, Greenmount, 30th June 1964*)

CHAPTER 5

Community Relations in Northern Ireland

From the earliest days of his premiership, one of O'Neill's main aims was to heal some of the ancient divisions in Northern Ireland between the Protestant majority and the Roman Catholic minority. Feeling that these divisions weakened the community and wasted much of its potential, he sought to convince those on both sides of the political-religious fence that they had much common ground. He went out of his way, by visiting Roman Catholic schools and other institutions, to demonstrate that he intended to be Prime Minister of all the people.

These policies were put to a severe test in 1966, when arrangements were being made by Republican sympathizers for extensive commemoration in Northern Ireland of the 1916 Easter Rising in Dublin. As plans for these celebrations advanced, tension in Northern Ireland mounted. The commemoration of what they regarded as a rebellion was widely resented by considerable sections of the population, and there were signs that extreme elements were prepared to express this discontent in a violent form.

The main commemorations of the Easter Rising were planned for the Easter weekend itself, and in these circumstances an invitation to O'Neill to address on Good Friday a joint Protestant-Roman Catholic Conference assumed unusual significance. The

Prime Minister used the occasion to define his attitude to community relations, and to make a notable plea for tolerance.

This Conference has been arranged in the spirit in which Easter ought to be celebrated in a Christian community. It is more concerned with our common Christianity than with our conflicting points of view. Such a meeting can do much good, and I consider it a privilege to be the first speaker.

But the Conference will not achieve its potential without frank speaking, and an admission of differences of principle. The avoidance of controversial issues may be comfortable, but it makes no real contribution to better understanding. In speaking frankly tonight, I am sure that I will offend no one here.

The Ulster community is a place in which two traditions meet—the Irish Catholic tradition and the British Protestant tradition. In India the place where two great rivers join together is often considered to have a particular sanctity—but it is also often a place of turbulence, as the currents from opposite directions swirl around each other.

By and large these religious traditions have also been synonymous with political views. This correspondence of religion and politics has, in the past, created certain peculiar frictions in our public affairs, and prevented us from mounting a united effort to surmount other social and economic problems.

A major cause of division arises, some would say, from the *de facto* segregation of education along religious lines. This is a most delicate matter, and one must respect the firm convictions from which it springs. Many people have questioned, however, whether the maintenance of two distinct educational systems side by side is not wasteful of human and financial resources, and a major barrier to the promotion of communal understanding.

One must face also the fact that political divisions become unusually sharp when the argument is not about means, but about ends. Thus, in most countries political parties differ merely about the methods to be used for the achievement of certain accepted national goals—economic stability and prosperity, higher living standards and so on. Disagreements of this kind admit the possibility of compromise. While the extreme positions, for instance, may be those of untrammelled private enterprise or complete state control, what in fact has emerged in the United Kingdom under governments of different complexion is a 'mixed' economy.

Here in Northern Ireland, however, disagreement has been centred not around the activities of the State, but around its very existence. Now it would be all too easy at a gathering such as this to speak soft words on this subject, and to give the impression that all that is needed to overcome every difficulty is goodwill. But that would be less than honest. I must say clearly that the constitutional position of Northern Ireland is not a matter on which there can be any compromise, now or in the future, and I must say, too, that I believe we have a right to call upon all our citizens to support the Constitution. The whole concept of constitutional government would be debased if the State were not to expect of its citizens at any rate the minimum duty of allegiance.

When I say that there can be no compromise on this issue, I have clearly in mind the welfare of *all* our people. In seven years as Minister of Finance, I came to know very well the inescapable logic of our financial arithmetic—the plain fact that any break in the British connection would condemn our community to an intolerable reduction in its living-standards.

Our political divisions of opinion will no doubt continue, but I would like to see them moved on to a new basis of rational argument. I have enough confidence in the economic and social advantages of my own political philosophy to be prepared to argue it on its merits, and without recourse to catch-cries or cheap slogans. I want the community to advance to achievements of which *all* its members will be proud. This has been my consistent aim as Prime Minister. I have spoken of the 'duty of allegiance' which the State expects; but I accept readily those obligations which the State owes in return.

I defer to no one in my readiness to practice and defend my own deeply-held Protestant beliefs, but I recognize and respect the rights of others to practice and uphold theirs. And all of us have a wider Christian duty to practice our religion 'with malice towards none, with clarity for all'.

One of our major difficulties is, that in an age of mass communications, the raucous sound of extremism is often heard much more loudly than the steady ground-swell of moderation. A bombing or a gimmicky demonstration provides a better headline or a more dramatic picture than the dignified expression of moderate opinion. This is a problem we have got to face, because no democratic society can afford to allow itself to be intimidated by violence or pushed around by noisy minorities. I can assure you that the Government intend to stand up to these people from whatever section of the community they may come—but it ought not to stop at that. I think there is also a job here for every organization of moderate opinion, and above all for the Churches.

There are certain challenges at certain times which must be met, whatever the cost. The *real* authority of the Christian Churches is a *moral* authority, and it is within their power to deploy that immense authority for the good of the community as a whole. The Government will speak clearly in terms of public order; I hope that the Churches will speak equally clearly in terms of moral order. Those who seek by word or deed to incite hatred and widen divisions in the community can be crushed by the universal disapprobation and distaste of decent people!

We in Ulster today have much to work for, and much to hope for. Last month's unemployment figure was the lowest for any March since the War, and our economy grows steadily stronger and better balanced. The physical development of the Province proceeds apace on every side. A great new industry has chosen our new City in County Armagh as the location for a massive factory. The Vice-Chancellor of our second university has been appointed, and planning is far advanced. Driving around Ulster, one encounters almost everywhere new or improved roads and motorways.

The future is full of promise for the people of Ulster. I believe that only two things can possibly stand in the way of full realization of that promise. One of these—a serious economic set-back for the United Kingdom as a whole—is not a matter within our control, although we can join our efforts with those of our fellow-citizens in defending ourselves against it. The other—which is very much within our own control—is the danger of self-inflicted wounds. It is easy to be impatient with the pace of change in 1966, but it is no answer to return to the mentality of 1926. We may not have achieved perfection in our affairs, but in the words of the song we are 'Forty years on', and have built up material and other assets which this generation must not squander.

If we cannot be united in all things, let us at least be united in working together—in a Christian spirit—to create better opportunities for our children, whether they come from the Falls Road or from Finaghy. In the enlightenment of education, in the dignity of work, in the security of home and family there are ends which *all* of us can pursue. As we advance to meet the promise of the future, let us shed the burdens of traditional grievances and ancient resentments. There is much we can do together. It must and—God willing—it *will* be done.

(*Corrymeela, 8th April 1966*)

In spite of the tense state of the country, the weekend of Easter

*1966 passed without undue incident. On the evening of 6th June,
however, incidents of violence occurred. A procession organized by
the extreme Protestant leader, Rev. Ian Paisley, was attacked by
Republican sympathizers while passing through a Roman Catholic
area of Belfast. The police, not without injury, protected the procession, which proceeded to picket—for its alleged 'Romanizing
tendencies'—the General Assembly of the Presbyterian Church,
the most numerous Protestant denomination in Northern Ireland.
In the course of this picketing the Moderator of the General
Assembly and a number of distinguished guests, including the
Governor of Northern Ireland, Lord Erskine, and Lady Erskine,
were subjected to noisy demonstrations and verbal abuse. A sense
of revulsion passed through the community, and in Parliament
O'Neill commented upon these events as follows:*

To those of us who remember the Thirties, the pattern is
horribly familiar. The contempt for established authority; the
crude and unthinking intolerance; the emphasis upon monster
processions and rallies; the appeal to a perverted form of
patriotism: each and every one of these things has its parallel
in the rise of the Nazis to power. A minority movement was
able in the end to work its will, simply because most people
were too apathetic or too intimidated to speak out. History
must not be allowed to repeat itself in this small corner of the
British Commonwealth.

The right of free speech is one of the most cherished elements of our democratic birthright. There is a healthy reluctance to curb the freedom which British citizens enjoy to
say even the most unacceptable things. That freedom is cir-
cumscribed only by the wider good of the community. Liberty
is guaranteed, but licence cannot be permitted. Dissent ought
to have untrammelled expression; but obscenity or sedition
eat away at the fabric of society.

In a place like Northern Ireland, where widely different

views are strongly and sincerely held by different sections of the community, freedom of speech and expression represents no danger to the health of the society, if two conditions are satisfied. First, that we are reasonably tolerant of the views of others. For generations, we have had a number of customary processions and parades, founded in tradition, and representing something of real significance to those who take part. They are an accepted part of our life. The second condition to be satisfied is this: that we should be able to express our own opinions and beliefs without being grossly offensive to others.

The vast majority of our people accept and understand these conditions. But those whose activities we are discussing today take a different view. While insisting upon their own unlimited right to free expression, they would deny it to others by the crudest forms of intimidation. They are not content with putting their own opinion, but resort to grossly offensive methods and language.

What we have to make unmistakably clear today is: who is to rule in Northern Ireland? Those of us who sit in this House have our political differences, but we have one great thing in common. Every single one of us, only a matter of months ago, entrusted our fortunes to the judgment of the people at a General Election. This is our unassailable authority to consider these matters, that we have come here in the democratic way to carry out the mandate which we have been given. We have not come here by false pretences; our record is known and we stand upon it.

This is a time for men and women to declare themselves, both in this House and beyond it. A great deal is at stake: our reputation in the world, our ability to continue to make material progress, our right to live in peace and harmony with each other and with our neighbours. It is a political issue, because we are called upon to assert the primacy of our democratic institutions. It is a moral issue, because intolerance, hatred, envy and uncharitableness are in all places and at all times evil things. It is a religious issue, because these things which have happened in our midst are alien to a truly Christian society.

There are hundreds of Ulster clergy who are devoted pastors caring for their flocks. Most of their names are not known to us, because instead of marching round and round Belfast in the hope of seeing their names in the paper, and ensuring that scenes of violence in Ulster will be seen not only in London and Edinburgh, but in Washington and Ottawa, they are quietly going about their Christian duty and instilling Christian principles into their congregations. On the Day of Judgment we in this House know to whom it may be said: 'Well done, thou good and faithful servant'.

I have said before, and I repeat it now, that the Government intends to keep the peace, without intimidation from *any* quarter. I am confident that this is what the House and the country would wish us to do. We will deal sternly with those who either give provocation or who respond to it with violence.

The Ulsterman has a reputation for commonsense. We have achieved a prosperity undreamed of even a few years ago. Is all this to be thrown away and replaced with street scenes tailormade for the television screens of the world? Public representatives at this time have a duty to show both dignity and courage, and an opportunity to display the qualities of true leadership. In a few weeks, Mr. Speaker, you and I with many others will remember with gratitude the soldiers of the Ulster Division who, fifty years ago at the Battle of the Somme, showed what real courage and real loyalty can be. Many in this House have already given a lead which is worthy of their memory. I hope and believe that others will do so today. Ulster demands our best. Let us be ready to give it.

(*House of Commons, 15th June 1966*)

But the grimmest events of a difficult year were still to come. Arrangements had been made to celebrate, on 1st July on the battlefields of Northern France, the 50th Anniversary of the Battle of the Somme, in which the 36th (Ulster) Division had fought so bravely and suffered so terribly in 1916. A few days beforehand, O'Neill flew to Paris to stay with the British Ambassador and meet French Ministers. On the early morning of Sunday 26th June, however, four young Roman Catholic men were fired upon in a Belfast street, leaving one dead and two injured. In the course of police inquiries leading to a number of arrests (and ultimately to convictions), clear evidence was discovered that a secret organization called the Ulster Volunteer Force had been formed to advance the cause of extreme Protestantism by violence. On Monday 27th June, O'Neill cancelled his programme in Paris and returned at once to Belfast to take charge of the situation. At a late-night meeting of Ministers, a decision was taken to use Special Powers legislation—hitherto only used against the I.R.A. and extreme Republican organizations—to proscribe the U.V.F. The following day, O'Neill announced this decision to the House of Commons.

The events which we discussed in this House on 15th June were, in all conscience, serious enough. But what we now have to consider is far more grave and grim. Human life has been wantonly taken. We are confronted by terrible acts which have shown no mercy to youth, no respect for old age. Our first duty in this House today is to condemn absolutely and without one shred of reservation this evil thing in our midst. To the relatives of those who have been killed and injured our utmost sympathy is due. Those who have lost their lives were our fellow-citizens. Violence against them was violence against us all.

I do not think the House will expect me to describe in detail the terrible events of early Sunday morning. It is enough to say that four young men were wantonly and wickedly attacked, leaving one dead and only one uninjured. Since then, police activity has been intense. Once again the Royal Ulster Constabulary have shown a thoroughness and efficiency to which proper tribute must be paid. During last night, two men were charged with the murder of Peter Ward and three men with the murder of John Patrick Scullion. Other charges have also been made, and nine men have appeared in court today, eight of whom have been remanded in custody. Police inquiries are continuing and further arrests are expected. The law will now take its course, and it is not for us to say anything which could prejudice the impartial verdict of justice. Nor do I think that prolonged further debate at this time would really serve the public interest.

The Government, however, is not prepared to let the matter rest there. Information which has come to hand in the last few days makes it clear that the safety of law-abiding citizens is threatened by a very dangerous conspiracy, prepared at any time to use murder as a weapon. This we cannot and will not tolerate. I said in this House on 15th June that 'the Government intends to keep the peace without intimidation from any quarter'. In fulfilment of that intention, my right honourable friend the Minister of Home Affairs has this morning made regulations under the Civil Authorities (Special Powers) Act (Northern Ireland), 1922, to declare an organization which has misappropriated the title 'Ulster Volunteer Force' an unlawful association.

As Honourable Members may know, I flew back last night from France. The purpose of my visit there was to honour the men of the 36th (Ulster) Division, many of whom were members of the authentic and original U.V.F. Let no one imagine that there is any connection whatever between the two bodies: between men who were ready to die for their country on the fields of France, and a sordid conspiracy of criminals prepared to take up arms against unprotected fellow-citizens. No; this organization now takes its *proper* place alongside the I.R.A. in the schedule of illegal bodies. We will not hesitate to act in a similar way against any other group or organization, however styled, which plans to do violence to the fabric of society.

I call upon those who may be connected with these people in any way to turn back before it is too late. One cannot touch pitch without being defiled. I warn those who set their ends before the interests of the community that the Government, acting in the best interests of all, will move against them with rigorous severity.

We stand at the crossroads. One way is the road to progress which has been opening up before us with all its promise of a richer and fuller life for our people. The other way is a return to the pointless violence and civil strife of earlier years. We must not let anyone push us down that road. For myself, I do not seek the political company of anyone who would condone or justify recent events in the slightest degree. I will not stand idly by and see the Ulster which we love dragged through the mud. Every person who has a shred of influence has a duty to use it wisely and responsibly. Above all else, I appeal for a spirit of calm and restraint. If we were to experience a series of reprisals and counter-reprisals, the consequences could be grave indeed for us all. The battle against these evil forces must be waged throughout the community; but it must begin here, in this House, today.

(*House of Commons, 28th June 1966*)

Firm action had its effect. Although the difficulties of 1966 were by no means at an end, communal violence of the most serious kind was averted. By the end of the year, in the Queen's Speech debate, O'Neill was in a position to look back in judgment and to draw conclusions.

When we look back upon 1966, while it has not lacked achievement, we cannot ignore incidents which inhibited our progress and disfigured our reputation throughout the English-speaking world, and indeed beyond. From one side came the extreme Republicans, who sought to flaunt before our people the emblems of a cause which a majority of us abhor, and who once again refused to renounce violence as a political weapon. From the other side came those self-appointed and self-styled 'loyalists' who see moderation as treason, and decency as weakness. Let us learn the lesson of these events and apply our energies, not to a rehearsal of the enmities of the past, but to an examination of the problems of the present and a realization of the opportunities of the future.

(*House of Commons, 13th December 1966*)

On 28th April 1967, in an article for 'The Times', O'Neill explained at length his approach to the problems of community relations in Northern Ireland.

It is a truism that Northern Ireland has long had a divided community. The reasons for this division are rooted in the long sequence of historical events connecting the destinies of Ireland and Great Britain. However those events may be interpreted, they do demonstrate with absolute clarity the fact that Irish problems are deep-seated and not amenable to facile external solutions, however well intentioned. When, by an irony of history, the one area of Ireland which had consistently resisted home rule was the only part left to operate a home rule parliament, it was unfortunate but perhaps inevitable that opinion polarized on a religious basis. This polarization tended to push both sides into extreme attitudes.

The majority, loyal by tradition and sentiment to its British heritage, regarded the minority as a disloyal 'Trojan Horse' in its midst, intent only upon subverting the constitution and merging Ulster in an independent All-Ireland Republic. The minority, seeing in the new Government merely a perpetuation of the historic Protestant ascendancy, withdrew into attitudes ranging from detachment to outright hostility. Northern Ireland simply cannot be understood unless it is appreciated that regularly over the years actual physical violence has been used as a political weapon: that as recently as 1956–62 a campaign of I.R.A. terrorism caused six deaths, thirty-four injuries and over £1 million worth of damage to property: and that for much of the period of the state's existence a substantial minority of its people have failed clearly to dissociate themselves from such activities.

At this point the reader may well comment that all too often in any discussion of Irish affairs one becomes lost in a lengthy historical preamble, long before reaching the present day. That is not my intention. I mention this background merely to put current events in their proper setting and perspective.

What was the position when I took office in 1963? The largest opposition party attending the Northern Ireland House of Commons, the Nationalist Party, had declined the role to which its numbers clearly entitled it, leaving a four-man Northern Ireland Labour Party to discharge the role of official opposition. Throughout society the hostility and suspicion of more than three decades still persisted very widely, although beginning to break down in more educated circles. This divide within society was paralleled by another in external politics, because not since partition had a Prime Minister of Northern Ireland met his opposite number in Dublin.

It was clearly time for a change, and the whole basis of my political effort of the last four years—with the help and support of my colleagues in the Government—has been to demonstrate that the historic divisions cannot be allowed forever to stand in the way of that community spirit without which we will never realize our full economic or social potential.

That is why I regretted so much in *The Times*' article, to

cite one example, the reference to Lord Craigavon's remark about 'a Protestant Parliament for a Protestant people'. This had some relevance in its historic setting of the troubled twenties, but it is no more representative of the present spirit of Ulster Unionist politics than the declarations of Stanley Baldwin are of conservatism in the sixties. What are the facts? By inviting the then Prime Minister of the Irish Republic, Mr. Sean Lemass, to Stormont I ended an absurd mini cold war and made possible a whole series of useful exchanges between Ministers on both sides of the Border. This did not mean any weakening whatever of Ulster's determination to remain within the United Kingdom, but it was intended on my part to create a more friendly and relaxed spirit both between the two countries, and within our own community. In our domestic policies over these recent years, we have consistently tried to emphasize those aims to which all our people can make a contribution, and from which no one will be excluded. I defy anyone to detect in our last election manifesto, or in any of the speeches in which my colleagues and I sought a further mandate, even a suggestion of a sectarian approach.

Little by little one had the impression that old barriers were in fact breaking down. Sensitive observers were able to detect a new and heartening aggiornamento in our affairs. Why, then, has the current critical attitude gained momentum? Unfortunately 1966 was not an easy year for us in Northern Ireland. There were widespread celebrations of the fiftieth anniversary of the Dublin Easter Rising, undoubtedly encouraged and exploited by people of extreme Republican views who would see in any permanent easing of inter-community relations a real threat to their ultimate aims. These celebrations in Belfast and elsewhere in their turn produced a backlash from the most extreme elements of ultra-Protestant opinion which had to be met by extremely firm action on the part of the Government of Northern Ireland.

These events made many people realize that harmony in a previously divided community cannot be achieved overnight, but demands a long and patient process of social and political education. *The Times* News Team commented on Monday, as though I had said something rather whimsical, that I had told them that 'Reform takes a long time'. Perhaps this illustrates the difference between the idealism of the journalist, who can propound his theories and leave for pastures new, and the realism of the politician, who has to cope with problems on the spot.

There are two points which must be made. First, that although reform does indeed take a long time—and is in fact a process which is never at an end in any community—no one should assume that reforms in Northern Ireland are not in progress. As an example, university representation and plural voting in elections to the Northern Ireland Parliament are being abolished, and we will be setting up a permanent impartial boundary commission to keep electoral boundaries under review. Ulster Members at Westminster have, of course, all along been returned for constituencies fixed by the U.K. Boundary Commission and on a franchise identical with that in Great Britain. Again, a most exhaustive re-examination of the functions, areas and financing of local government is now under way, and this is likely to lead to far-reaching reforms in that area.

The second point to make is that many of the criticisms now being directed at us are demonstrably ill-founded. We have been accused, for instance, of 'discrimination' in the siting of Ulster's new city and second university; yet in both these instances we were guided by the most objective expert advice—in the one case Sir Robert Matthew, and in the other a committee chaired by Sir John Lockwood, neither of whom had any connection with Northern Ireland or was influenced in any way by the Northern Ireland Government.

Of course there are still some unhealthy tensions in Northern Ireland affairs, although comments equating the lot of the Ulster Catholic with that of the American Negro are absurd hyperbole. But there really is no acceptable or truly democratic alternative to letting us find the solution for our own problems. Stormont is, after all, a democratically elected Parliament, and no solution which is imposed upon the majority of the population could fail to provoke greater evils than it would solve.

I would like to conclude by quoting some words I used at Easter last year, when, at a time of considerable strain, I spoke to a joint conference of Protestants and Roman Catholics. I said:

'It is easy to be impatient with the pace of change in 1966, but it is no answer to return to the mentality of 1926. We may not have achieved perfection in our affairs, but in the words of the song we are "forty years on", and have built up material and other assets which this generation must not squander. If we cannot be united in all things, let us at least be united in working together—in a Christian spirit—to create better opportunities for our children, whether they come from the Falls Road or from Finaghy [a Roman Catholic and a Protestant area, respectively]. In the enlightenment of education, in the dignity of work, in the security of home and family there are ends which all of us can pursue. As we advance to meet the promise of the future, let us shed the burden of traditional grievances and ancient resentments. There is much we can do together. It must and—God willing—it will be done.'

It is my hope that, in spite of the current clamour, my colleagues and I may be allowed to pursue the course inherent in these words. Certainly this is not the moment for an ill-judged intervention in our affairs. As I said at the beginning, the long history of Anglo-Irish relationships warns that such an intervention may produce effects which no one can foresee. What we want to do is not to become involved in a profitless exchange of charge and counter-charge but to emphasize more and more those things which unite Protestant and Catholic in our community. For, in the last resort, a truly happy and stable society must depend not upon legislation by Stormont or by Westminster but upon mutual trust.

('*The Times*', *28th April 1967*)

In February 1968, O'Neill was invited to address the Irish As-sociation in Belfast. He used the occasion for his most comprehen-sive review of community relations since the 'Corrymeela Speech' of 1966.

As we go further along this road of improved community re-lations, what should be our aim? First of all, let us discard the unrealistic. The *Irish Times* in a recent editorial expressed the hope that one day the North would embrace the heritage of Robert Emmett and Wolfe Tone. This is the kind of wishful thinking which for too long has held back the sane tide of reality in Irish affairs. Anyone who thinks the Protestant com-munity in Northern Ireland is ever going to embrace the G.A.A., the Irish language, and the Fenian Brotherhood is being about as realistic as someone who expects one day to see a banner of Queen Victoria carried in a Hibernian parade.

Then we have people, genuinely trying to be helpful, who advocate a kind of reciprocal emasculation. No National An-them or Loyal Toast to offend one side; no outward signs or symbols of Nationalism to offend the other. This approach, too, I believe to be misconceived; it is rather like trying to solve the colour problem by spraying everyone a pale shade of brown. Moreover, as I said at Corrymeela, and I think it bears repeating:

'I believe we have a right to call upon all our citizens to

128

support the Constitution. The whole basis of constitutional government would be debased if the State were not to expect of its citizens at any rate the minimum duty of allegiance.'

I expect, therefore, neither total surrender of one point of view to another, nor a sweeping under the carpet of major differences on points of principle. What I see is rather an occupation of a broad area of middle ground by reasonable men and its steady widening in the course of time.

The people of this island are often accused of brooding unduly over the events of the past. 1690 and 1798, Cromwell and King James, Wolfe Tone and Lord Randolph Churchill—such occasions and personalities are popularly supposed to be seldom out of their minds. But is this really true? The people of England have a considerable sense of history, and a varied chronicle to which they can apply it, but who seriously imagines today that the Sussex farmer or the plater on Tyneside dwells upon Nelson or Wellington, Magna Carta or the Reform Bill? They are far more concerned with the value of their take-home pay, with job stability, with the education of their children. I think the idea that people on this side of the Irish Sea have some different motivation is a myth which ought to be exposed. If the publicists and the politicians and the propagandists were to mute their historic trumpet calls, who would call for a reprise when the last note had died away? This was very much what I had in mind as long ago as 1964 when—in the course of one of those cross-Border exchanges, now a thing of the past—I said:

'Both Mr. Lamass and I will show our patriotism in a much more relevant way by striving to better the lot and increase the prosperity of the people within our respective jurisdictions.'

In the discussions of the Economic Council, in the work of the Industrial Training Boards, and indeed in the great majority of all the issues which confront a modern government, the terms 'Catholic' and 'Protestant' are not really relevant. They are particularly irrelevant in the local, civic setting. This is why I attach such importance to the series of Civic Weeks associated with the programme which I have called 'a Programme to Enlist the People', or P.E.P. for short. Whether one calls it Derry or Londonderry, surely one wants one's native city to grow and prosper. In a better Ballynahinch there will be more opportunities for all its inhabitants. New industries for Newry mean new hope for all its people. It is hardly surprising that some of the most offensive picketing to which I have been subjected was in the context of a Civic Week, because the makers of mischief see in this upsurge of harmony a strong antidote to their policies of prejudice, division and malice.

I have spoken of a broad area of middle ground which can be occupied by reasonable men. If there is to be a continuing movement in that direction, I think the community as a whole ought to be giving rather more thought than it does to the complex of activities in which its members are engaged.

A great many of the elements in our society—institutions, clubs, organizations, associations—are organized on a denominational basis, in form or in fact. Now there is absolutely nothing wrong with this; why should not like-minded people wish to meet and act together?

But at the same time I wonder whether it would not be possible for organizations to reach out, in some of their activities, across denominational barriers. After all, qualities like charity, civic concern, and interest in the problems of the young, the old or the handicapped, are universal in their nature.

In the post-War era, the idea of 'twinning' between cities here and those in foreign countries—some of them our enemies in World War II—has been widely developed. It has, I think, made a useful contribution to good feeling within the international community. Coming closer to home, I have myself some knowledge of the twinning of Chambers of Commerce in Castlebar and Ballymena, with mutual benefits in terms of greater knowledge and respect.

I would like to see this concept of 'twinning'—and the idea of friendly interchange and co-operation which underlies it—promoted very widely across the barriers which custom has erected here at home. This could only be done by the voluntary initiative of men and women of goodwill. People talk of building bridges as if it were a matter of a single crossing of the historic river of tradition and sentiment and loyalty which divides us. But the barrier represented by this great river is not one which can be nullified by a single bridge. Those who confront each other from the opposite banks must rather build their own bridges, with their own materials and in their own locations.

I believe there is particular scope for this co-operation across denominational boundaries in the field of voluntary effort for the good of the community. Voluntary Service Overseas receives a proper acclaim; but voluntary service at home could serve not only its own ends of service, but the wider cause of communal understanding.

Is it, for instance, too visionary to look forward to Protestant young people helping to re-decorate a Youth Club in Andersonstown, or a young Catholic reading to a bed-ridden old lady on the Shankill Road? The firmest links can only be forged at the basic level of ordinary, warm, human contact.

I have emphasized advisedly the role which youth might, indeed must, play. In the final resort, the only satisfactory answers to the problems we are discussing lie in their hands. In their impatience with our shortcomings lies the best hope for the future of this country.

(*The Irish Association, Belfast, 19th February 1968*)

In June 1968, the Prime Minister was invited to open a Hall erected as a memorial to a young Constable, W. J. Hunter, who had been killed in an I.R.A. outrage some years ago. O'Neill's theme (which undoubtedly rose also from the recent assassination of Senator Robert Kennedy) was the ultimately self-defeating character of violence.

In dedicating this Hall, and in keeping his memory green, I am sure none of us seeks to keep old enmities alive or to re-open old wounds.

Let this monument to him rather stand as a symbol—and a peculiarly fitting one at this time—of the utter emptiness of violence as a political weapon. Again and again it has been proved that it is the cause of the victims, and not that of the perpetrators, which benefits by such terrible acts.

Moreover, violence so heedless, so senseless, so irresponsible tends to unite men of goodwill from different backgrounds in a determination to shun the methods of the gunman.

(Opening of W. J. Hunter Memorial Hall, Coleraine, 7th June 1968)

Unfortunately, Northern Ireland had further violence to endure. On 5th October 1968, a 'Civil Rights' demonstration was held in Londonderry, which led to a violent confrontation with the police. The scenes which occurred were widely reported around the world, and British public opinion was deeply concerned. Mr. Harold Wilson invited Captain O'Neill to meet him to discuss these events.

O'Neill, while convinced that some part in this explosion of violence had certainly been played by extreme elements hostile to Northern Ireland's constitution and Government, was quick to acknowledge that it would not have been possible without the existence of genuine social evils—evils, indeed, whose existence he had long appreciated, and for which he had been seeking solutions.

His first act after the Londonderry disturbances was to summon to a special Housing Conference representatives of every local authority in Northern Ireland. There he emphasized to them the need not only to keep up the pace of the housing programme, especially in areas of social need, but to adopt methods of allocation by which justice would not only be done, but be seen to be done. There was to be an early and significant response to his words when the Corporation of Londonderry decided to change its system from personal allocation by the Mayor to a points basis.

On 15th October, the events in Londonderry were discussed in the House of Commons. In his speech, O'Neill used these words:

What have been presented as years of stagnation have in fact been years of immense economic and social progress—progress in whose benefits Protestant and Roman Catholic alike have shared. Our Government, caricatured as an inflexible and unreasonable autocracy, has not only accepted desirable change but urged it.

But I must warn those who seek to impose changes upon us by violence or other forms of coercion that there is no course of action less likely to commend their cause to a majority of our people. In the last resort, change has to be *acceptable* change. Living happily together in a mixed community depends not upon legislation but upon a growth of trust and confidence. Neither internal violence nor attempts to engineer outside pressure is likely to promote such trust or encourage such confidence.

For more than five years I have been trying to improve relations between the two sections of the community. What happened last weekend has certainly set us back a bit, but I will continue to hope, and to work, for better times ahead. But if we have further violence, further disorder, there will inevitably be on both sides a retreat into traditional attitudes, and the slender bridges men of goodwill have tried to build will tumble into a chasm. If these bridges should fall, many years may pass before they could be built again. Above all else, at this critical moment, we want a pause, a period of calm, an interval of restraint in word and action. This to my mind at the present time is more important than anything else.

This very day there is being published the results of a National Opinion Poll conducted amongst the young people of Northern Ireland—the seventeen to twenty-four age-group. They were asked at one point to place in order of priority the things which they considered the Government should do. The result of this Poll, conducted in a calm atmosphere before the events in Londonderry, is revealing. It shows that their first priority is a demand for more industry to be brought to the Province. The second request is for more houses. And such things as alleged discrimination and the franchise, which form the political catch-cries of politics, come far behind.

Here are our young people asking us for bread—for the bread of jobs and houses, a decent prosperous life—and are we to offer them instead the stone of discord? For unless the Province rapidly returns to sanity, future progress is gravely at risk. I call above all for peace. The place for political argument is in Parliament, not in the streets. Disorder is the way not to equal rights, but to an equal share of misery and despair.

(*House of Commons, 15th October 1968*)

But as agitation continued, O'Neill felt it necessary to remind Ulstermen of their obligations as citizens of the United Kingdom.

The Unionist Party holds power to win for the people of Ulster a growing prosperity and a respected place in the life of the United Kingdom. It should not be necessary to state this. At every Election we have proclaimed 'Ulster is British'. These are the words which we have placed above our Party Headquarters as the central slogan and symbol of Unionist thinking. They have been the pith and substance of every manifesto on which we have fought a General Election.

It is no new theme. Few recall today, though they are worth remembering, the words of King George V when he opened our first Parliament nearly half a century ago. He expressed his confidence:

'... that the important matters entrusted to the control and guidance of the Northern Parliament will be managed with wisdom and moderation, with fairness and due regard to every faith and interest, and with no abatement of that patriotic devotion to the Empire which you proved so gallantly in the Great War.'

Wisdom; fairness; patriotism—those are the three qualities which the King commended to us—not for a single Session or a single Parliament, but as the continuing watchwords of our State.

Now what does the situation demand of us today? It demands, surely, that we should persevere with the task of winning for the present constitutional position of Ulster the support of the widest cross-section of the people of Ulster. And it demands, too, that we should seek to buttress that position with the continued sympathy and understanding of the people and parties of Great Britain.

When we had a General Election in 1965, we set out in our Manifesto a programme designed to appeal to every citizen. It was not so much an ideology as a prospectus, inviting all our people to make an investment in the future. It contained no grand, empty phrases but business-like proposals for jobs and houses and schools and hospitals. Polling Day showed that these are the things which matter to people, and public opinion polls have since affirmed it. We have a formula here, not for a partisan success but for the grand design of a broadly-based Ulster. We were saying to people: come out of the morass of political and sectarian dissension in which we have been sunk for too long and build with us on new and higher ground.

That appeal met with a violent reaction from the assorted extremists in our community not because it was failing, but because it was beginning to succeed. If you have fed upon discord for generations, harmony seems a starvation diet. And if we allow recent events to frighten the moderate men in our community into a retreat from the middle ground, then we will have presented a cheap victory to the engineers of those events. The motive force of statesmanship has to be more than a reflex reaction.

Moreover, the course we have steered over the last few years has been one acceptable in direction—if not always in speed—to the people and parties of Great Britain. I can tell you with complete conviction that there would be no support or sympathy whatever for any attempt to reverse that course.

What we have got to realize is that we enjoy an extremely privileged position within the United Kingdom. Not only have we the right—within certain constitutional and financial limits —to conduct our own affairs in our own way, but we have the most generous financial support of the nation as a whole to enable us to do so. It is not always appreciated that our Constitution alone—the 1920 Act as amended—is not of itself a passport to prosperity. If we had been given the 1920 Act and nothing but the 1920 Act, we would not be enjoying our present British standard of life and services, but a lower Irish standard.

But we should not imagine that our present privileged position is accepted by everyone in Great Britain without a degree of envy. After all, there are other parts of the United Kingdom, with economic problems not dissimilar to ours, which have to accept the policies Whitehall thinks best and make do with a good deal less financial assistance than we receive.

However, by and large the British people have been happy

to accept our special position for a number of reasons. First of all, the 'Irish question' was a painful issue in British politics for a great many years. People generally were glad to be rid of it and to let the Parliament established in the only remaining British part of Ireland get on with its job. Secondly, our war-time conduct won us many friends, as compared with the neutrality of the South—but we must accept, I fear, that as these events fade from the memory so also does the sentiment of gratitude. Thirdly, we have been seen to conduct an efficient administration, to which the chief threat has been external violence.

These circumstances have changed to our disadvantage. Very skilfully the 'Irish question' has been brought once again on to the Westminster stage. Post-War loyalty and sentiment count for much less than they did, especially amongst the young. And the picture is being presented not of external attack, but of internal dissension.

Now I would consider any re-appraisal of our position within the United Kingdom to be very dangerous. Although our financial dependence is self-evident to anyone who thinks about these things at all, my fear is not just one of a less generous financial arrangement. No; my chief fear is rather that the economic, the financial and the political are all so closely inter-related that a reconsideration of one inevitably affects all.

How do we meet this danger—for it is a danger? By showing Britain and the world that all Ulstermen have a real part to play in our institutions; by demonstrating for all to see that there is respect here for the rights and aspirations of every citizen. Where greivances and complaints are ill-founded and rooted in malice, let us be eager to expose the truth. But if social, economic or political grievances are well-founded we could do no better than to act in the spirit of Lord Craig-avon's first full-scale speech to the new Northern Ireland Parliament, when he pledged:

'. . . to have our Parliament well established, to look to the people as a whole, to set ourselves to probe to the bottom those problems that have retarded progress in the past. . . .'

In this, as in other things, let us be the true heirs of Craigavon, and so strengthen our position with the United Kingdom that we will be able in 1971 to celebrate our Golden Jubilee in security, in harmony and in a prosperity undreamed of by Carson and Craigavon.

'Ulster will fight, and Ulster will be right' is a declaration familiar to every Ulsterman. But for what was Ulster ready to fight then, and for what ought she be prepared to fight today? For the Union—that bond of loyalty and sentiment and common concern—which has made us since the early days of the Nineteenth Century citizens of the United Kingdom. Our status of government—let it be remembered—is not Home Rule but devolution. Stormont came into being not as an alternative to Westminster but as part of a new pattern to cement the Union more firmly than ever before. I have said before, and I repeat it now, that the policy of our Government is to maintain Northern Ireland as an integral and respected part of the United Kingdom. We cannot maintain Northern Ireland in a vacuum. We must in practice be a part of the United Kingdom or a part of an Irish Republic. Let us never forget that in rejecting the second course we necessarily adopted the first.

So if Ulster fights for those things which will strengthen her as a part of the United Kingdom, then—and only then—will she be right.

It may be that Westminster and Whitehall have never intervened against our will in our domestic affairs; but merely to state this is to be unjust to the work of successive British Governments, whether Conservative, Coalition or Labour. Let us recall how we went to Whitehall to discuss the problems of Ulster farmers and came back with the Remoteness Grant; how we urged the difficulties of Shorts and received finance for the Belfast and the Skyvan; how we argued the needs of Harland and Wolff, and not only received aid to stave off liquidation, but were enabled to provide at Queen's Island facilities second to none in Europe.

Whenever there is a labour dispute and a great industry works to rule, we realize that society could not function if we worked according to the book. And if Westminster and White-hall were ever to work to rule—giving us our strict entitlement under Statute Law and nothing more—every man, woman and child in Ulster would rapidly feel the pinch.

Let us have an end to talk about the United Kingdom as if it were some hostile and remote power. This is the whole of which we in Ulster are a part. This is the great nation which has underwritten our march to progress over nearly half a century. If we in Ulster do the job which has to be done—keeping in our minds the three words, wisdom, fairness and patriotism which I mentioned at the beginning—we need fear no intervention, no interference, no constitutional crisis. We can look instead to a continuation of that co-operation, that generous assistance, which the people of Britain have so freely given us. But if we should fail to live up to our responsibilities, then in due course the people of Ulster would rightly condemn us for all we had put at risk.

For myself, my duty is clear and I propose to do it. Nor, when the issues are appreciated, can I doubt that this strong and historic Party will show the greatness to marry firmness in defence of the law with magnanimity and tolerance. In doing so, it will be true to its finest traditions, and worthy of the trust which, as successive Elections, our people have placed in it.

(The Unionist Society, 28th October 1968)

On the 4th November Captain O'Neill and two of his colleagues met Mr. Wilson and the Home Secretary for discussions on the Northern Ireland situation, and on 22nd November the Government announced far-reaching reforms, including the appointment of a statutory Development Commission to accelerate the development of Londonderry, new action to secure demonstrably fair housing allocation, the appointment of an Ombudsman, and, abolition of the company vote at local government elections. These changes were accepted by the Unionist Parliamentary Party.

Nevertheless, the situation remained potentially explosive. On 30th November, in Armagh, the police had been fully stretched to keep apart 'Civil Rights' demonstrators and a large element opposed to them. With rising feelings on both sides of the sectarian and political divide, O'Neill felt it necessary to appeal directly to the body of moderate opinion which had been largely silent. This appeal was broadcast on television on the evening of 9th December, and is probably O'Neill's best-known speech, broadcast as it was all over the world.

Ulster stands at the crossroads. I believe you know me well enough by now to appreciate that I am not a man given to extravagant language. But I must say to you this evening that our conduct over the coming days and weeks will decide our future. And as we face this situation, I would be failing in my duty to you as your Prime Minister if I did not put the issues, calmly and clearly, before you all. These issues are far too serious to be determined behind closed doors, or left to noisy minorities. The time has come for the people as a whole to speak in a clear voice.

For more than five years now I have tried to heal some of the deep divisions in our community. I did so because I could not see how an Ulster divided against itself could hope to stand. I made it clear that a Northern Ireland based upon the interests of any one section rather than upon the interests of all could have no long-term future.

Throughout the community many people have responded warmly to my words. But if Ulster is to become the happy and united place it could be there must be the will throughout our Province and particularly in Parliament to translate these words into deeds.

In Londonderry and other places recently, a minority of agitators determined to subvert lawful authority played a part in setting light to highly inflammable material. But the tinder for that fire, in the form of grievances real or imaginary, had been piling up for years.

And so I saw it as our duty to do two things. First, to be firm in the maintenance of law and order, and in resisting those elements which seek to profit from any disturbances. Secondly, to ally firmness with fairness, and to look at any underlying causes of dissension which were troubling decent and moderate people. As I saw it, if we were not prepared to face up to our problems, we would have to meet mounting pressure both *internally*, from those who were seeking change, and *externally* from British public and parliamentary opinion, which had been deeply disturbed by the events in Londonderry.

That is why it has been my view from the beginning that we should decide—of our own free will and as a responsible Government in command of events—to press on with a continuing programme of change to secure a united and harmonious community. This, indeed, has been my aim for over five years.

Moreover, I knew full well that Britain's financial and other support for Ulster, so laboriously built up, could no longer be guaranteed if we failed to press on with such a programme.

I am aware, of course, that some foolish people have been saying: 'Why should we bow the knee to a Labour Prime Minister? Let's hold out until a Conservative Government returns to power, and then we need do nothing.' My friends, that is a delusion. This letter is from Mr. Edward Heath, and it tells me—with the full authority of the Shadow Cabinet and the expressed support of my old friend Sir Alec Douglas-Home—that a reversal of the policies which I have tried to pursue would be every bit as unacceptable to the Conservative Party. If we adopt an attitude of stubborn defiance we will not have a friend left at Westminster.

I make no apology for the financial and economic support we have received from Britain. As a part of the United Kingdom, we have always considered this to be our right. But we cannot be a part of the United Kingdom merely when it suits us. And those who talk so glibly about acts of impoverished defiance do not know or care what is at stake. Your job, if you are a worker at Short's or Harland & Wolff; your subsidies if you are a farmer; your pension, if you are retired—all these aspects of our life, and many others, depend on support from Britain. Is a freedom to pursue the un-Christian path of communal strife and sectarian bitterness really more important to you than all the benefits of the British Welfare State?

But this is not all. Let me read to you some words from the Government of Ireland Act, 1920—the Act of the British Parliament on which Ulster's Constitution is founded.

'Notwithstanding the establishment of the Parliament of Northern Ireland . . . the supreme authority of the Parliament of the United Kingdom shall remain unaffected and undiminished over all persons, matters and things in [Northern] Ireland and every part thereof.'

Because Westminster has trusted us over the years to use the powers of Stormont for the good of all the people of Ulster, a sound custom has grown up that Westminster does not use its supreme authority in fields where we are normally responsible. But Mr. Wilson made it absolutely clear to us that if we did not face up to our problems the Westminster Parliament might well decide to act over our heads. Where would our Constitution be then? What shred of self-respect would be left to us? If we allowed others to solve our problems because we had not the guts—let me use a plain word—the guts to face up to them, we would be utterly shamed.

There are, I know, today some so-called loyalists who talk of independence from Britain—who seem to want a kind of Protestant Sinn Fein. These people will not listen when they are told that Ulster's income is £200 million a year but that we can spend £300 million—only because Britain pays the balance.

Rhodesia, in defying Britain from thousands of miles away, at least has an Air Force and an Army of her own. Where are the Ulster armoured divisions or the Ulster jet planes? They do not exist and we could not afford to buy them. These people are not merely extremists. They are lunatics who would set a course along a road which could only lead at the end into an all-Ireland Republic. They are not loyalists but *dis*loyalists: disloyal to Britain, disloyal to the Constitution, disloyal to the Crown, disloyal—if they are in public life—to the solemn oaths they have sworn to Her Majesty The Queen.

But these considerations, important though they are, are not my main concern. What I seek—and I ask for the help and understanding of you all—is a swift end to the growing civil disorder throughout Ulster. For as matters stand today, we are on the brink of chaos, where neighbour could be set against neighbour. It is simple-minded to imagine that problems such as these can be solved by repression. I for one am not willing to expose our police force to indefinite insult and injury. Nor am I prepared to see the shopkeepers and traders of Ulster wrecked and looted for the benefit of the rabble. We must tackle root causes if this agitation is to be contained. We must be able to say to the moderate on both sides: come with us into a new era of co-operation, and leave the extremists to the law. But this I also say to all, Protestant or Roman Catholic, Unionist or Nationalist: disorder must now cease. We are taking the necessary measures to strengthen our police forces. Determined as we are to act with absolute fairness, we will also be resolute in restoring respect for the laws of the land.

Some people have suggested that I should call a General Election. It would, in my view, be utterly reprehensible to hold an Election against a background of bitterness and strife. I have spoken to you in the past about the groundswell of moderate opinion. Its presence was seen three years ago when we fought an election on a Manifesto which would stand inspection in any Western democracy and we swept the country on a non-sectarian platform. Those who would sow the wind by having a bitter Election now would surely reap the whirlwind.

And now I want to say a word directly to those who have been demonstrating for Civil Rights. The changes which we have announced are genuine and far-reaching changes and the Government as a whole is totally committed to them. I would not continue to preside over an Administration which would water them down or make them meaningless. You will see when the members of the Londonderry Commission are appointed that we intend to live up to our words that this will be a body to command confidence and respect. You will see that in housing allocations we mean business. You will see that legislation to appoint an Ombudsman will be swiftly introduced. Perhaps you are not entirely satisfied; but this is a democracy, and I ask you now with all sincerity to call your people off the streets and allow an atmosphere favourable to change to develop. You are Ulstermen yourselves. You know we are all of us stubborn people, who will not be pushed too far. I believe that most of you want change, not revolution. Your voice has been heard, and clearly heard. Your duty now is to play your part in taking the heat out of the situation before blood is shed.

But I have a word too for all those others who see in change a threat to our position in the United Kingdom. I say to them, Unionism armed with justice will be a stronger cause than Unionism armed merely with strength. The bully-boy tactics we saw in Armagh are no answer to these grave problems: but they incur for us the contempt of Britain and the world, and such contempt is the greatest threat to Ulster. Let the Government govern and the police take care of law and order.

What in any case are these changes which we have decided must come? They all amount to this: that in every aspect of our life, justice must not only be done but be *seen* to be done to all sections of the community. There must be evident fairness as between one man and another.

The adoption of such reforms will not, I believe, lose a single seat at Stormont for those who support the Unionist cause and indeed some may be gained. And remember that it is with Stormont that the power of decision rests for maintaining our Constitution.

And now a further word to you all. What kind of Ulster do you want? A happy and respected Province, in good standing with the rest of the United Kingdom? Or a place continually torn apart by riots and demonstrations, and regarded by the rest of Britain as a political outcast? As always in a democracy, the choice is yours. I will accept whatever your verdict may be. If it is your decision that we should live up to the words 'Ulster is British' which is part of our creed, then my services will be at your disposal to do what I can. But if you should want a separate, inward-looking, selfish and divided Ulster then you must seek for others to lead you along that road, for I cannot and will not do it. Please weigh well all that is at stake, and make your voice heard in whatever way you think best, so that we may know the views *not* of the few *but* of the many. For this is truly a time of decision, and in your silence *all* that we have built up could be lost. I pray that you will reflect carefully and decide wisely. And I ask all our Christian people, whatever their denomination, to attend their places of worship on Sunday next to pray for the peace and harmony of our country.

(Television broadcast on B.B.C. and I.T.A. networks,
9th December 1968)

The response to O'Neill's solemn and sincere appeal was phenomenal. At once telegrams and letters of support began to flow into Stormont Castle, and in the weeks which followed nearly 150,000 people (out of a total population of under one and a half million) signed messages or declarations endorsing the sentiments of the television speech. Two days after it had been made, O'Neill also sought the support of his Party colleagues in the House of Commons, and received an overwhelming vote of confidence.

The 'Civil Rights' leaders declared a period of truce; but this was broken at the beginning of January 1969, when the 'People's Democracy', a group based largely on Queen's University, Belfast, undertook a march from Belfast to Londonderry. This march was opposed at a number of points on the route, and there was further violence both on the march and in Londonderry after it had reached its destination. On 11th January the 'People's Democracy' arranged another demonstration in the town of Newry, which degenerated into indiscriminate rioting.

On 15th January, the Northern Ireland Cabinet announced further measures to take the heat out of the situation: the appointment by the Governor of an impartial Commission to investigate the disturbances and their causes, coupled with a strengthening of the law dealing with processions and demonstrations. In the days which followed, demonstrations planned by opposing factions were cancelled.

CHAPTER 6

Self-Help: Ulster Weeks and P.E.P.

Self-help was one of the major themes of O'Neill's 'Pottinger speech' as early as 1962. His administration has been notable for two principal overtures in this field. The first of these was the launching of a series of 'Ulster Weeks' in the major cities of Great Britain, beginning with Nottingham in October 1964. These Weeks have covered the promotion of Ulster's manufactures and agricultural products, and also of tourism. They have been a joint venture between business and government of a unique kind, and have forged quite new links between Northern Ireland and the major centres of population in Great Britain.

Captain O'Neill's speech in Nottingham exemplifies his approach to this project.

In three ways, we in Northern Ireland make a major contribution to the life of Britain. First, our diversified industrial production contributes to national wealth and to the export drive. So-called 'Irish linen'—virtually all of which is in fact produced in Ulster—is a major dollar earner throughout North America. Both our industrial production and our productivity have been growing in recent years at a rate well above that of Britain as a whole.

Secondly, I want you to think of us as one of Britain's key food suppliers. Those of you who enjoy bacon and eggs for your breakfast may not realize it, but according to the last reckoning we were sending you each year over £18 million worth of bacon and ham, and nearly £12 million worth of eggs. Altogether, we were shipping to Great Britain agricultural products to a total annual value of over £63 million.

Thirdly, I would like you to think of us as a great, largely untapped playground almost on your doorstep. Across that little strip of water, which need present no terrors today, are endless miles of wonderful motoring on roads where another car is an event; sandy beaches stretching as far as the eye can see, uncluttered and unspoiled; lake country to match Windermere, still waiting to be enjoyed; heath and mountain and forest; streams full of fish. It is, perhaps, our own fault that we have not yet developed fast enough as Britain's playground. That is now being remedied, and new hotels or improvements to existing ones are springing up here, there and everywhere.

Northern Ireland as a workshop of Britain; Northern Ireland as a larder of Britain; Northern Ireland as a playground of Britain: these are three roles which we are able to play. But I do not want you to think of us entirely in impersonal terms. We would like you to come to know us as people, as your fellow-citizens in this great nation in whose interests we work together. How is your Ulsterman made up? He is certainly part soldier, because Ulster has been a veritable nursery of field-marshals: Alexander and Montgomery, Templer and Alanbrooke and Dill all came from the North of Ireland, and we are proud to have nurtured such men. He is a man to whom this country, its traditions and its place in the world mean a great deal. He is a determined enemy, and a good and loyal friend.

We have come here to sell you our goods, to show you what we can produce, to tell you what we can offer to the industrialist, the tourist or the casual visitor. I think that is a good foundation for a continuing relationship, because people who do business with each other come to understand each other better.

But this is not an effort confined to trade, or limited to the bounds of a single week. We want to make friends as well as customers, and to forge links with you which will endure.

(*Civic Lunch, Nottingham, 26th October 1964*)

Out of this venture in external self-help there developed another, internal movement. It has come to be called P.E.P. ('a Programme to Enlist the People'). Its origins are to be found in a speech by the Prime Minister to a conference of local authorities in October 1966.

May I use this occasion to throw out another positive suggestion? As you know, some two years ago we launched our campaign of Ulster Weeks in Great Britain, partly as an exercise in good will and partly for their trade value. Now it is, of course, very right and proper that we should make the maximum effort to sell our goods outside Northern Ireland. But our own local market of $1\frac{1}{2}$ million people is not to be despised. Some towns in Ulster have been organizing Civic Weeks, and I believe that many more would do so if it could be demonstrated that they were giving a boost to the progress of Ulster as a whole.

What I have in mind is that in future locally organized civic weeks might be supported by mounting displays of Ulster goods in the shops in the same way as in Ulster Weeks in Great Britain, and also by using the excellent photographic exhibition showing the growth of Northern Ireland which forms a centrepiece of our Weeks across the water.

Civic Weeks should help develop not just civic pride, but the active interest of the community in what is happening around them and in the Province at large. What I would like to see, therefore, is a whole series of voluntarily organized

Community Weeks held in all the larger centres of population in Northern Ireland, to show our own people that 'Ulster can make it', to convey the real significance of modern development to every part of the Province, and to emphasize the importance of individual effort and individual commitment.

If this idea is acceptable to local opinion, I am prepared to have it raised with the Committee which runs our Ulster Weeks, to see what help they could give. But I must emphasize that I do not think such an exercise would be worthwhile if run and wholly financed by the central Government. What I would like to do is rather to encourage existing local effort.

(*Conference of local authorities, Portrush, 20th October 1966*)

The response was such that, in opening a Belfast 'Ulster Week' in January 1967, O'Neill was able to use the following words.

We are, I hope, launching a new movement in Ulster, which might be called P.E.P.—a Programme to Enlist the People.

This movement stems from two developments. One is the successful series of Ulster Weeks which we have mounted in Great Britain. Not only have we brought a wide range of Ulster-made goods and farm products to the shops of a series of great British cities; but we have conveyed a new striking picture of life in Ulster today, and—perhaps most important of all—linked together a substantial number of Ulster businessmen in a co-operative venture designed to help each of them *and* the Province as a whole.

The other development upon which these events are based is the very successful Civic Weeks which various towns have launched over the last year or two.

Thinking about these things, I began to wonder why we should not demonstrate the products of Ulster, and the development of Ulster to our *own* people, and whether the Government could not somehow encourage the Civic Weeks movement and turn it—in the interest of Northern Ireland as a whole—into something bigger and more important.

I therefore suggested, at a Local Authorities Conference held in Portrush last October:

'a whole series of voluntarily-organized Community Weeks . . . in all the larger centres of population in Northern Ireland, to show our people that "Ulster can make it", to convey the real significance of modern development to every part of the Province, and to emphasize the importance of individual effort and individual commitment.'

The response to this suggestion has been quite excellent. Today, we are launching the Belfast Ulster Week to be held in May. It will open with the Lord Mayor's Show and the Royal Ulster Agricultural Society's Centenary Show and Pageant will take place in the latter part of the Week. Leading stores have already promised to mount displays of Ulster goods, and there will be many other events. This encouraging story will be repeated in many other places. Limavady, Downpatrick, Antrim, Newry, Coleraine and Londonderry have already made plans for Weeks this year, and I hope other towns will join in next year. I will do my best to visit as many of these events as I can.

What is vitally important in all this is that it is not—and should not be—a central Government venture. The whole point is to encourage the people of each city or town in a spontaneous expression of civic pride, and in developing a new sense of involvement in what the Province as a whole is doing.

Modern life and the activities of government become more complicated every day, and it is small wonder that the man in the street often feels baffled, frustrated or confused. We in the Government believe that what we are doing to improve the quality of life in Northern Ireland is right, but all too often the citizen is aware of these activities only when they hurt him. Yet, in the long run, real and sustained progress is impossible in a democracy unless you can persuade people to take an active and informed interest, and carry them with you. Traditional methods are not enough. They have been tried and found wanting.

P.E.P.—our Programme to Enlist the People—must have two parts: one, Tell the People; two, Involve the People. In the interests of telling the people, we are getting together an Exhibition, which will be available to as many 'Ulster Week' towns as possible and which will, we hope, help to answer the question: 'What does development—what do motorways, New Towns, more university places, physical and economic planning, mean to me?' Because these are difficult times financially, this Exhibition will not be very large or elaborate. But it does not need to be either of these things. It will aim to get away from jargon and bureaucratic complications, and to tell the average Ulsterman what 'building the new Ulster' actually means.

The other leg of our programme is to Involve the People. There is a place here for every organization which is capable of making an effort for the public good. I have in mind very much the position of youth. I have never shared for one moment the disapproving opinions which some people seem to hold about our younger generation. Irreverent, yes, questioning certainly, but also full of energy and idealism which we do not harness often enough. I know, for instance, that the boys of a Belfast school recently laid on a shopping expedition for hundreds of old and disabled people. All over Ulster, I believe that there are young people who want to be committed, and who lack only the opportunity.

But this is not confined to youth or youth organizations. There is a place here for organizations like Chambers of Commerce, Rotary Clubs, the Council of Social Service, Road Safety Committees. There is a very big place indeed for the Churches, who will I hope within this setting consider working together in some field of public benefit.

Ulster Weeks in our towns will be the most obvious example of P.E.P. in action but I want to see it as a continuing thing, not just as something which lasts a week and then peters out.

Some Jeremiahs may say: is this difficult economic period the right time to launch such a venture? My reply is that there will never be a better time. Self-help and self-reliance represent an engine which can help to get us moving again. Let us enlist the people in support of the efforts of central and local government and the business community. Let us show the world just what Ulster can do.

Later the Prime Minister explained the purposes and the philosophy of P.E.P.

I believe that if you want to commit the people of a town, or a region, or for that matter the whole country to some renewed effort, there are two things you must do. First, you must *tell* the people. Secondly you must *involve* the people. The State, and the organs of government both central and local, are involved today in issues so complex that only a minority of people understand them. Perhaps this did not matter a hundred years ago, when power was the perquisite of a small privileged class, and when newspapers had the space to print—and their readers the time to digest—detailed accounts of lengthy Ministerial speeches. But today we live in a world in which the people as a whole have power, and in which major issues are summarized, headlined and presented for easy consumption by the mass audience. Is it any wonder that so many major issues pass over people's heads, that they feel no involvement? And yet I also believe that throughout this country there are rich sources of community spirit waiting and indeed imploring to be harnessed. Take youth as an example. If our young people sometimes stray into foolish or frivolous paths, is it not because their elders have failed to harness the latent idealism which, given half a chance, they demonstrate so convincingly? Would it not be a terrible indictment of all our modern educational and social development if we were producing thereby an inferior generation of young people. But I do not believe this; I totally deny it. Indeed, just as the post-war generation is stronger physically, so too I believe it has the potential to be stronger intellectually and morally.

This is the thinking behind a new movement which we have launched in Ulster, and which I have called P.E.P.—a Policy to Enlist the People. Its purpose is to inform and involve the people in the development of the community, within the setting of their own city or town. Over the next couple of years, towns throughout Northern Ireland will be having community weeks. They will feature displays of Ulster goods in the shops, so that our own people can feel a proper pride in their achievements. There will be a Government exhibition of modern developments, bringing to each town the story of what new motorways, new towns, new industries mean in human and individual terms. There will be activities designed to draw in, and to involve every aspect of a town's life—its local Council, its Chamber of Commerce, its trade unions, its voluntary, sporting, charitable and youth organizations. We hope young people will do something positive—whether it is clearing up a derelict area, or visiting old people and decorating their homes, or taking invalids shopping. And we call all this P.E.P. because we believe it will be a tonic to civic and community spirit, that it will help to bridge the gulf between 'us', the people and 'them', the Government, that it will make people understand that it is their country and cannot be developed without them.

(*Nottingham Chamber of Commerce, 7th March 1967*)

CHAPTER 7

Relations with the Irish Republic

One of the most sensitive issues of Northern Ireland politics has always been the question of relations with her Southern neighbour, variously known over the years as the Irish Free State, Eire and the Irish Republic. The Government of Ireland Act, 1920, which remains the basis of Northern Ireland's Constitution, had set out to solve the Irish question by establishing two Irish Parliaments, one in Northern and one in Southern Ireland, within the United Kingdom. The Act provided for ultimate union of the two Parliaments, in the event of Northern Ireland so deciding. However, this constitutional settlement was unacceptable to majority opinion in Southern Ireland, where a de facto Sinn Fein Government had come into being. In 1921 the United Kingdom Government negotiated with this de facto leadership a treaty establishing an Irish Free State with dominion status. Northern Ireland, however, was given an option to retain its existing status, and this was swiftly exercised. In 1925 the existing boundary line between Northern Ireland and the Irish Free State was confirmed by an agreement between the London, Dublin and Belfast Governments.

However, with the return to office of the party led by Mr. De Valera, which had never accepted the 1921 treaty and had indeed precipitated a Civil War in the South, relations between Northern Ireland and the Free State deteriorated. The promulgation of a new Constitution laying claim to the whole of Ireland was un-

acceptable to majority opinion in Northern Ireland, and a series of assaults by I.R.A. terrorists, often operating from Southern territory, did not assist the development of a cordial relationship. Southern Irish neutrality in World War II, and the declaration in the South in 1948 of a Republic outside the Commonwealth, merely widened the estrangement. Moreover, between 1956 and 1961 a further wave of terrorist outrages occurred.

Nevertheless, the two Governments in Ireland did not remain totally at arm's length. In practical matters, such as Erne drainage and the problem of the Great Northern Railway, the two Governments in the post-war period negotiated and conducted mutually useful agreements. There had, however, been no meeting of the respective heads of Government since Cosgrave and Sir James Craig had met when the Agreement of 1925 was being prepared. The question of recognition was the major stumbling block. On the Northern side, it was argued that de jure recognition had been accorded by agreement in 1925, and that it was flying in the face of reality to withhold it. On the Southern side, the accordance of such de jure recognition appeared to be outside the realm of immediate practical politics, given the views of the major parties on 'Partition'. As O'Neill's premiership began, it remained to be seen whether any accommodation was possible.

In late July 1963, De Valera's successor as Prime Minister of the Irish Republic, Sean Lemass, went some cautious way towards resolving the impasse. In a speech at Tralee, referring to Northern Ireland, he recognized that 'the Government and Parliament exist with the support of the majority . . .'. Although O'Neill, replying at Cookstown in September, reiterated the established Unionist view on the desirability of full constitutional recognition, he ended with an appeal for a concentration upon more immediately relevant issues.

In October, however, during the course of a visit to the United States, Mr. Lemass called for the ending of the partition of Ireland in terms which drew a firm rebuke from O'Neill.

During 1964 there were no dramatic developments in North–South relations; but the comparison between the flexible pragmatism of Mr. Lemass and the rigidity of his predecessor began to create a more favourable atmosphere.

However, on Thursday, 14th January 1965, the news was released that, at Captain O'Neill's invitation, Mr. Lemass had travelled to Belfast and was lunching with him at Stormont House, his official residence. Afterwards the following joint communiqué was issued:

We have today discussed matters in which there may prove to be a degree of common interest, and have agreed to explore further what specific measures may be possible or desirable by way of practical consultation and co-operation. Our talks—which did not touch upon constitutional or political questions—have been conducted in a most amicable way, and we look forward to a further discussion in Dublin.

On 3rd February, in the course of a Parliamentary debate, the Prime Minister outlined reasons for inviting Mr. Lemass to Belfast.

I asked Mr. Lemass to meet me because I believed such a meeting would be in the best interests of Northern Ireland.

Our Constitution, as I said in the House after my meeting with Mr. Lemass, and as this Motion reiterates, is not in doubt. Let me remind hon. Members of what is laid down in the Ireland Act passed at Westminster in 1949:

'It is hereby declared that Northern Ireland remains part of His Majesty's dominions and of the United Kingdom and it is hereby affirmed that in no event will Northern Ireland or any part thereof cease to be part of His Majesty's dominions and of the United Kingdom without the consent of the Parliament of Northern Ireland.'

I have never, at any time, disguised my view that it would be useful to call a halt to meaningless long-distance arguments about Partition. Our position on this is perfectly well known and so is that of the Republic. Our people have demonstrated at successive elections where their loyalties lie. So what is the use of continuing to talk *ad infinitum* about an issue which is not open to negotiation? As long ago as October 1963, I said in a speech at Newcastle:

'Let there be an end to public statements, either in Ireland or abroad, about the "ultimate reunification of our country", "the evils of partition", "the Six-County area", and similar subjects. I do not suppose that Mr. Lemass or his colleagues will change their personal opinions on these subjects overnight. They, equally, must have realized by now that I do not intend to change mine.'

On the other hand, as I said at Londonderry about a year ago:

'It was never intended that, under the Government of Ireland Act, there should be anything but a purely *political* boundary between North and South.'

And I pointed out in a Statement which I issued in September 1963, that:

'It has been demonstrated in the past that there is no bar to specific co-operative measures, provided these are of clear mutual benefit, have no political or constitutional undertones and can be carried out within our limited powers.'

I have quoted these various remarks, made throughout my period of office, to show that I have consistently and publicly advocated a policy of friendliness and co-operation, subject always to the protection of our constitutional position.

I attach less importance to pieces of paper than to actions. And I came to the conclusion that if Mr. Lemass was prepared to drive through the gates of Stormont and to meet me here as Prime Minister of Northern Ireland he was accepting the plain fact of our existence and our jurisdiction here.

What do I expect from the meeting with Mr. Lemass? I do not anticipate any sudden or dramatic economic benefits. These must continue to come very largely from our association with the British economy, and it would be mere wishful thinking to imagine otherwise. In the field of trade, we must realize that external trade is handled on a United Kingdom basis and that in any case it is the Republic whose tariff barriers are the main obstacle to cross-Border trade. Having said all this, however, it is always worthwhile to seek benefits for our people, even if they prove to be limited. And I can see no reason why, in certain matters, useful steps by way of practical co-operation should not be taken. Constitutional and political questions will, of course, continue to be ruled out.

In any case, the benefits for which I look are not entirely, or even mainly, practical. It would be my hope that, if relationships can be conducted on a sane and reasonable level, policies of hatred and violence will make less and less appeal. Moreover, a degree of co-operation in practical matters should promote better knowledge of the people on the other side of the Border. Many of the myths about Northern Ireland current in the South are misconceptions based upon ignorance. People who know nothing of our affairs at first hand can believe, quite sincerely, that the separate existence of Northern Ireland enjoys little support here and that it would collapse tomorrow but for the presence of the British Army. If such people really know us, they would see that things were otherwise. They might not welcome our constitutional attachment to Britain any more than they do now; but at least they would understand it.

We in Ulster have nothing to hide and nothing to fear. I believe that, because of my invitation to Mr. Lemass, Northern Ireland stands higher in national and world opinion than ever before. Let us show that our loyalties are rooted not in obstinacy but in principle; not in bigotry but in fidelity. Let us extend the hand of friendship to our neighbours, confident in our strength as an integral part of the United Kingdom. *(House of Commons, 3rd February 1965)*

Later in February, O'Neill paid a return visit to Dublin, and a series of inter-departmental and inter-Ministerial discussions on matters of common interest got under way. However, the Prime Minister made it very clear that this attitude towards purely practical co-operation did not mean any weakening of Ulster's opposition to any change in its constitutional status. Irish Nationalism, in his view, had nothing to offer the people of Northern Ireland.

The result of the Northern Ireland General Election of 1965, held within months of the historic meetings with Mr. Lemass, was for O'Neill a striking endorsement of the new approach in North–South relations, as in so many other matters.

Nevertheless, remarks continued to be made from time to time, both in Dublin and in London, which made desirable a definition of Ulster's position.

Thus, in January 1967, the British Prime Minister, Mr. Harold Wilson, while attending a meeting of the Council of Europe in Strasbourg, was asked by a member of the Irish Republic's delegation to comment on the prospects of Irish unity within an extended European Economic Community. Mr. Wilson replied at some length. In the course of this reply he said:

It is a problem for the people of Ireland. I know, just as my predecessors, that no one would be happier than Great Britain if this problem is solved by agreement within the Emerald Isle.

However, when questioned by Mr. Rafton Pounder, M.P., an Ulster Unionist member of the United Kingdom delegation, Mr. Wilson confirmed that it remained the policy of the British Government to abide by the provisions of the 1949 Ireland Act in relation to the constitutional status of Northern Ireland.

The following month, O'Neill referred to these exchanges.

I said in the House of Commons recently that—while I regarded the process of discussion, consultation and agreement with the Republic on economic issues of mutual benefit, and with no strings attached, as a useful and enlightened process— a constant reiteration of outworn anti-Partition sentiments would make no contribution to that process whatever.

Since then, statements made in the Dail, particularly by Mr. Aiken, have underlined my remarks in an unfortunate way. These statements can be answered only by a strong reaffirmation of our own constitutional position, and before we know where we are we have returned to the old cross-Border long-distance slanging contest, of which all sensible people are sick and tired. This is the way to drive rational co-operation for the common good out of the window. I would be sorry to see the position degenerate once again into the old state of ideological 'cold war'. It is often forgotten that in December 1925 the Governments in London, Dublin and Belfast joined together in an Agreement. The Preamble of that Agreement expressed a desire:

'to avoid any causes of friction which might mar or retard the further growth of friendly relations'

between the Government and peoples of the three Parties, and Article 5 declared that:

'the Government of the Irish Free State and of Northern Ireland shall meet together as and when necessary for the purpose of considering matters of common interest . . .'.

Unfortunately that Agreement was followed by many regrettable developments, and the 'causes of friction' were multiplied rather than reduced. Nevertheless we have made a sincere attempt, over the last couple of years, to 'meet together as and when necessary'.

Is it, I wonder, possible that now, forty-two years later, we might all take account of modern developments and 'avoid any causes of friction' for the future? There would be no need to shed genuine aspirations or renounce basic principles, but rather to face facts and get away from the cant and humbug which have long characterized this whole issue.

What is the nub of the matter? It is that anyone with a trace of practicality knows perfectly well that a basic change in the status of Northern Ireland could not be brought about by coercion. The attempt to do so once almost brought the United Kingdom to the brink of Civil War. In the spirit of modern times, such a thing could not even be attempted. A vigorous and self-reliant community of a million people cannot be treated as a chattel to be passed from one proprietor to another.

The responsible people in Dublin know this perfectly well. They know that for all the talk about the unification of Ireland, any 'unity' which would leave a great disgruntled and dis-affected minority would create far more evils than it would solve. I know that a few pathetic gunmen think otherwise. They imagine even now that a million Ulstermen ánd women can be cowed and bludgeoned into unwilling submission. But they are a spent force, and responsible people in Dublin can best bring about their final demise not by appearing at times to compromise with them, but by openly repudiating and con-demning their views.

As a result of Mr. Harold Wilson's remarks at Strasbourg, some Southern politicians think they have detected some new declaration of policy—that Partition would not be imposed by Britain in circumstances where the Republic and Northern Ireland wished to end it. But what is new about this? Even the most facile study of history shows that the British Govern-ments, when the Irish Free State came into being, afforded every opportunity for Northern Ireland to go into the Free State, had its people so wished. But, very properly and very realistically, there was no question of coercing the Northern Ireland people against their will as clearly declared in Parliament.

Is it not clear that if the United Kingdom Government would not wish to maintain a status which Northern Ireland did not want, neither—as a corollary—would it seek to change the existing status as long as Northern Ireland wished to maintain it? This has been the position since the Ireland Act of 1949. Is it not clear that when the Government of the Republic reaffirm their hope that one day Northern Ireland may wish to join the Republic of her own free will, they ought also to agree that the only appropriate and democratic way in which that free will could be expressed would be by the consent of the Parliament of Northern Ireland?

And is it not clear above all that, believing as we do that Ulster's best interests will always lie in the British connection, we must affirm that this status rests upon the consent of our people as expressed in Parliament?

Only upon this basis of realism can a policy of friendly consideration of matters of mutual interest be sustained. And on such a basis we would have nothing to fear from it. Because I talk to my neighbour in a friendly way across the garden fence, and perhaps even agree that we should share some gardening tools with him, it does not mean that I intend to let him live in my house.

I say these things today not to create controversy, but to clear the air. We cannot allow Northern Ireland's attitude to be misrepresented in any quarter. I ask you all to play your full part in setting the record straight. We are not perfect, and where there are genuine grounds for reform, your Government will not be slow or reluctant to act. But let it be clear that we are not amenable to pressure or misrepresentation. We will do our duty as we see it in the interests of all the people of Ulster. No one will divert us from that course.

(*Annual Meeting of Ulster Unionist Council, Belfast,*
24th February 1967)

As the question posed to Mr. Wilson at Strasbourg indicated, there were those who looked for a change in the constitutional position of Northern Ireland if and when both the United Kingdom and the Irish Republic were to be admitted to membership of the European Economic Community. O'Neill, however, strongly contested this argument.

In my view, then, those who see Europe as the setting for a united Ireland are following the old, time-worn course of self-delusion. Let me say it quite clearly and firmly, for all the world to hear and understand: Ulster—whether within the European Community or outside it—will remain British because that is the freely expressed political will of its people. If the United Kingdom enters Europe, it is as a part of Britain that Northern Ireland will make—I hope—a useful and distinctive contribution to the life of that wider Community.

Of course, if both the United Kingdom and the Republic join the Community, the sensible co-operative measures between North and South, which help us both and do no constitutional damage to Ulster whatever, will take on added value. Since overall competitiveness will be more vital than ever, savings—for example, on the cost of electricity supply will be extremely useful. I see no reason why contacts and co-operation should not be extended, provided that it is clearly understood that we made such contacts and participate in such co-operation as a part of the United Kingdom.

(*House of Commons, 14th November 1967*)

Nevertheless, in spite of the need for occasional clarification, the policy of neighbourly cross-Border relations continued to prosper. There were further meetings at the highest level between O'Neill and Lemass's successor, Jack Lynch, and by the end of 1967 the Prime Minister was able to express the hope that future meetings would be regarded as normal and indeed routine.

I believe the vast majority of sensible people are delighted that the two Governments can openly co-operate on matters of mutual concern. Now that this meeting has taken place, I am confident that the community as a whole will in future show sufficient maturity to treat further meetings as wholly routine and unremarkable, as indeed they are likely to be. No service is done to the cause of good cross-Border relations by attaching to meetings at any level a feeling of false drama.

(*House of Commons, 17th December 1967*)

Unfortunately the civil disturbances in Northern Ireland towards the end of 1968 again put the cross-Border relationship under some strain. Mr. Lynch publicly declared that partition was the root cause of these disorders, while one of his Ministers, Mr. Blaney, made remarks about Northern Ireland which were deeply resented. O'Neill therefore thought it essential to explain to a wider public the nature of relationships between North and South. For his forum he chose an audience of British Members of Parliament at a meeting of the Commonwealth Parliamentary Association.

People do not always recall today that for many, many years Ireland was one of the great issues—indeed the paramount issue before the British Parliament. Here was a topic which made and unmade Ministries, which divided and convulsed great parties, which frustrated and embittered the life of Parliament and led this nation very close indeed to the brink of Civil War.

For many years now that great issue has receded from the centre of the stage. But no one should underestimate its dangerous and explosive implications, and it behoves all of us as public men—whether in Great Britain, in the Irish Republic or in Northern Ireland—to weigh our words carefully, to be guided by facts not by emotions, and to be responsible in our actions.

The current interest here in Northern Ireland's affairs, the recent comments by Mr. Lynch—the Irish Republic's Prime Minister—on Partition, and the impending establishment of a Commission on the Constitution; all these made me feel that it is my clear duty to inform the British Parliament, and through them the British people, of Northern Ireland's present attitude to major constitutional issues. In the present situation, a major misjudgment of this attitude could have very serious consequences.

I must begin with a little history. It is often said that in Ireland we are prisoners of our history, but clearly some brief reference to it is necessary to set the scene. You will be relieved to hear, however, that we can by-pass Strongbow and even the Battle of the Boyne to arrive at the Nineteenth Century.

There is an Irish version of the course of Anglo–Irish relations, from Mr. Gladstone's First Home Rule Bill onwards, which might be summarized somewhat as follows: 'There was never', they insist, 'any real willingness on the part of English politicians to concede any worthwhile element of self-rule to the Irish. Ultimately it became clear to them that it would be impossible to maintain the British position throughout Ireland, but instead—by a cynical manœuvre—they artificially divided the island and created conditions for continued British rule in a restricted area.'

I believe this to be a misstatement of the historical facts. It is absolutely true that many British politicians wanted to preserve the existing Union, because they believed this would be in the best interests of all, including the Irish. And looking back on it now, can we doubt that wiser statesmanship might have preserved the link between two sister islands with so much in common?

But as it became more and more clear that Ireland must be given some form of self-rule, the attitude of the people of Ulster began to emerge as a fact of life. Stubborn, irritating, determined Ulster existed; no one had to create it. There was no cynical plot involved, unless you attribute to King James I in the early years of the seventeenth century a quite remarkable gift for long-term planning. Right or wrong, wise or foolish, high-principled or merely stubborn—you can form your own judgment of the views of Ulster in the years leading up to 1914. But this, I say, is beyond dispute, that they were *authentic* views, held by people who were indeed ready, if the need arose, to 'put these grave matters to the proof'. And gradually British politicians of every complexion came to realize that the coercion of Ulster was impossible; that you could not utterly change the constitutional position of these very determined people against their will.

And so we come to the statute on which Northern Ireland's constitution is still founded—the Government of Ireland Act, 1920. It was a well-meaning compromise between the views of those in the South of Ireland who wanted complete detachment from Britain, and the views of those in the North who were determined to remain British, come what may. It established two devolutionary Parliaments—one in Dublin and one in Belfast—with powers of internal Government; it retained the link with Westminster through Irish Members from both North and South; and it provided a framework for the unification of Ireland if both sides should so decide.

Ulster accepted that settlement and determined to work it. She had never sought a Parliament of her own, but accepted it as part of a general settlement retaining the link with Britain. The South did not accept it. Even the establishment of an Irish Free State, retaining very tenuous ties with the Crown, involved a bitter Civil War in the South. And by slow degrees a State was created there whose policies and outlook were entirely alien to the majority of Ulster people.

However, from 1922 onwards the country which is now called the Irish Republic and was then known as the Irish Free

State, had complete control of its own destiny. It had a Government responsible to a parliamentary majority and with a legitimate claim to make agreements on behalf of its people. And now I come to a point which is often conveniently forgotten. In December 1925, the Governments in London, Dublin and Belfast concluded an Agreement, freely entered into on all sides. The Preamble expressed a desire

'to avoid any causes of friction which might mar or retard the further growth of friendly relations'

between the Governments and peoples of the three Parties, and the Agreement, which was confirmed by each Parliament, confirmed the boundary line between North and South as enacted in 1920. Those who are interested will find Westminster's confirmation in the Ireland (Confirmation of Agreement) Act, 1925.

The point I want to make is that the lawfully constituted Government of the Irish Free State accepted, in free agreement, both the Border and the existence of a legitimate Parliament and Government in Northern Ireland.

The Dublin Government was headed in those days by a wise, modest, and responsible statesman, Mr. Cosgrave, and I have little doubt that his policies would have led in time to steadily improving relationships between North and South. Unhappily for the future of North–South relations, he was succeeded in 1932 by Mr. De Valera—by a new party with new policies. I realize I am speaking now of one who is President of a friendly country, and who in his venerable age has come to be acknowledged as one of the most remarkable and enduring political figures of our time. But in him, the mystic and the visionary have always been to the forefront. Because he had a dream of an Irish-speaking Ireland, he ignored the fact that the vast majority of his people spoke only English. Because he had a vision of Ireland united, he could not see that there were people who had loyalties of another kind.

Under his leadership Eire closed its eyes to the realities of the situation, ignored the Agreement of 1925, and promulgated in 1937 a new Constitution laying claim to the whole island of Ireland, including the area within the jurisdiction of the Northern Ireland Government.

Moreover, by defaulting on its treaty obligations to the British Government, the Government of Eire initiated the so-called 'trade war', and erected on the Border a high tariff barrier. This, I emphasize, was no part of the settlement of 1920. The British Isles could have retained—and indeed did for the first period after partition—the characteristics of a Customs Union. It was Eire, not Northern Ireland or the United Kingdom, which gave to the Border the nature of an international customs frontier. For many years now, most goods passing from Eire to the North have continued to come into the United Kingdom duty-free. Not so, however, trade passing in the other direction. The manufactures of many Ulster firms, including those which have a natural hinterland in the South, have been excluded by insuperable tariffs or other forms of protection. In time, the Anglo–Irish Trade Agreement will end this situation, but as of today it still persists.

Is it surprising that such attitudes were resented in Northern Ireland? Is it remarkable that when we also had to endure physical violence from I.R.A. terrorism, strongly based in the South, people in Northern Ireland took the view that these people were not interested in friendship or co-operation, but in imposing a settlement on us by force or other forms of coercion? Eire's neutrality in World War II did nothing to bridge the deep gulf of sentiment and tradition. And finally in 1948—with Mr. De Valera out of power, and a new Coalition Government in office—there came the declaration of an Irish Republic, and the final, irrevocable breach with Britain and the Commonwealth.

When that occurred, the Northern Ireland Government of the day very properly pressed for a clarification of its constitutional position from Mr. Attlee's Government. This clarification was given, in two respects, and there should be no ambiguity about its nature.

It is not often that an Act of Parliament makes a solemn declaration on a major constitutional issue; but when it does so, the declaration of Parliament is, in my view, uniquely serious and binding. So may I read to you Section 1(2) of the Ireland Act, 1949.

'It is hereby declared that Northern Ireland remains part of His Majesty's dominions and of the United Kingdom and it is hereby affirmed that in no event will Northern Ireland or any part thereof cease to be part of His Majesty's dominions and of the United Kingdom without the consent of the Parliament of Northern Ireland.'

That declaration is not only solemn and binding, but it is also realistic. For how could a basic change be made in the constitutional status of Northern Ireland against the will of those who have been chosen—and fairly chosen, as I shall show in a moment—to represent its people in its own Parliament?

But the matter does not end there, for in addition to the statutory declaration of Northern Ireland's territorial integrity Mr. Attlee pronounced a wider-ranging guarantee of her right to constitutional self-determination. He said in the House of Commons on 28th October 1948:

'The view of H.M. Government has always been that no change should be made in the *constitutional status* of Northern Ireland without Northern Ireland's free agreement.'

Mr. Harold Wilson was a member of the Government which gave that pledge, and on at least three occasions—the latest on Wednesday 30th October 1968—he has reaffirmed it. The Conservative Party also accept it as a pledge binding any Conservative Government. The very clear inference is that there ought not to be any major change in constitutional arrangements affecting Northern Ireland which would be unacceptable to it. And I really feel I ought to make this clear beyond all possible doubt. If the United Kingdom Government and the United Kingdom Parliament were to make a declaration tomorrow in favour of a United Ireland, it would achieve nothing really practical within Ireland. The choice must clearly be between a union by coercion—which I suggest to you is even more unthinkable now than it was in 1912; a union by consent—and let there be no doubt that we in Ulster do *not* consent to it; or an acceptance of the position as it actually exists. Do not be deceived by the slogans demanding that England should get out of Ireland. We *have* an Irish Government in the North. My colleagues and I are Irishmen too; but our crime in Southern Irish eyes is that of being Irishmen who are loyal to the Crown, and to a constitutional union with Britain which has embraced us for over 150 years. Please remember that what is now Northern Ireland was part of the United Kingdom when Nelson fought at Trafalgar and Wellington at Waterloo; that we were British before the nationhood of most members of the United Nations had even been thought of; that you are asking us to accept that men like Alexander or Alanbrooke or Templer should not have considered themselves British. I say again—we cannot and will not consent to this.

Since we are talking here of Northern Ireland's consent, I would now like to consider the validity of the Parliament of Northern Ireland as a means for expressing that consent. First of all, with extremely minor exceptions, the franchise for Elections to Stormont, our local Parliament, has been on the same basis of universal adult suffrage as for Elections to Westminster. There are 4 University seats out of 52, and there is a business vote accounting for 12,954 on the present Electoral

Register of 925,041. Both the business vote and the University seats are to be abolished under legislation now passing through our Parliament, but in any case neither of these features has had any appreciable effect upon the outcome of any Northern Ireland Election.

There is, of course, another element in determining the outcome of Elections—the distribution of seats. These could be organized in such a way as to lead to under-representation of certain elements in the community. Indeed they could, and an impartial observer would have to agree that there *are* some undue disparities between the sizes of constituencies for the Northern Ireland Parliament. Electorates vary between 3 of under 10,000 and 2 of over 40,000; but the 15 seats with the largest electorates are *all* held by Unionists, mainly very comfortably, while 4 of the 6 with the smallest electorates are held by Opposition parties. Mr. Gerry Fitt, for instance, represents the tiniest electorate in Northern Ireland at Stormont. At the last Ulster General Election his *poll* of 3,326 votes in an electorate of 7,620 compared with 14 Unionist *majorities* of more than 3,000 in average electorates of almost 23,000. I report this to you not to introduce a political issue, but to demonstrate that Ulster General Elections, far from over-stating the will of the electorate on the constitutional position, have if anything been muting it. This is confirmed by forgetting about seats won, and looking at total votes cast. At each successive General Election, candidates who support the existing constitutional position have greatly out-polled all others—even though many Unionist candidates are at each Election returned unopposed.

So I want you to be in no doubt about the will of Ulster, which has time and again been declared and affirmed in the democratic way.

Now what is our attitude today, to the Irish Republic on one hand and Great Britain on the other?

In 1965, in spite of the continued unwillingness of Southern politicians to face up to the actual position in Ulster, I decided to take the initiative of meeting the then Dublin Prime Minister, Mr. Sean Lemass. I knew he was a hard-headed realist, prepared to recognize the realities of the situation, and I regarded our meeting as a *de facto*, if not *de jure* recognition of Northern Ireland. We agreed from the start to set political and constitutional issues on one side, and concentrate instead upon promoting economic and other forms of practical co-operation—in tourism, in power supply and so on. This was the basis—the sensible, realistic basis—of my two meetings with Mr. Lemass and my subsequent two meetings with his successor, Mr. Lynch. I knew, of course, that they retained in their hearts the wish for a united Ireland; but they, too, knew that I retained my loyalty to the United Kingdom. What I must emphasize is that, from my point of view, the object of such talks was to promote a decent, sane neighbourly relationship. Canada is no less an independent country and a member of the Commonwealth because of her friendly links with America.

But if such a relationship is to flourish, it demands sensible restraint and common prudence. You cannot go on talking business with someone who comes blundering into your back garden, kicking over the plants. Mr. Lynch can have a friendly relationship based on mutual respect, or he can have the luxury of allowing himself to intervene in the domestic affairs of Northern Ireland and the United Kingdom. He really cannot have both.

For we are British, and determined to remain British. We value our British citizenship, and are prepared to take the rough with the smooth in exercising it. You will have heard, and it is true, that Ulster—like other poorer regions of Britain —receives assistance from central funds. But there were years when taxation was high and our public expenditure small, and when we made a very large contribution to the central Exchequer. During the wartime period, from 1939–40 to 1944–5, the tax revenue of Northern Ireland was some £200 million, and of this over £131 million was retained by the Exchequer as our contribution to Imperial expenditure. These, too, were the years when we endured Nazi air attack and the other hardships of war at your side.

Your British citizenship has never been threatened, as ours has been. If at times we seem to you stiff and defensive, it is because constant attacks have been made upon all that we hold most dear. Not only verbal attacks, unfair as some of these may have been, but also physical brute force, exercised by armed bands of I.R.A., based in the Republic, whose forays into our territory as lately as 1956–62 led to the burning of Customs posts, armed assaults on police stations and army camps, the cowardly murder of six members of our police force, and damage to property amounting to over £1 million. The perpetrators of these acts always openly stated that their aim was to force Northern Ireland into an Irish Republic. Through all this long period of provocation, be it noted that the Ulster people did not once retaliate, angered and grieved though they were. What we ask in Northern Ireland is to be allowed to make up our own minds about our own destiny. That is enough. That is all we seek. We do not intervene in the domestic affairs of the South of Ireland. No terrorist bands from the North have sought to coerce the South. Leave us in peace, and there will be peace—peace in which the Governments in Ireland, North and South, may get on with the things which really matter. For our part, let me declare in conclusion that as long as I am Prime Minister it will be my aim, and that of my Administration, to build in Ulster a just and prosperous society, in which all its citizens may play a full and equal part. In all things it is our intention to see that justice is done and is seen to be done. Give us your continued help from Westminster, and there is no problem beyond our power to solve in time. Let us work together to house the homeless, to find work for the unemployed, to heal ancient grievances and make Northern Ireland the happy, harmonious, progressive community it can be.

(Commonwealth Parliamentary Association, Westminster, 4th November 1968)

CHAPTER 8

Northern Ireland and the United States

Terence O'Neill has always had a particularly deep interest in promoting the ties of kinship and common interest between Northern Ireland and the United States. He first visited the U.S.A. when attending in 1959, as Minister of Finance, the World Bank meeting in Washington. As Prime Minister he has paid numerous further visits. He is the first Ulster premier to have been received by a President (Lyndon B. Johnson) at the White House, and he has met many other leading American figures, including Vice-President Hubert H. Humphrey and the late Senator Robert F. Kennedy.

At the Bullock Forum in New York, O'Neill spoke of Ulster's 'special relationship' with America.

There has been a great deal of argument and discussion lately in Britain about education in business management. It is not surprising, therefore, that an intense spotlight has been focused upon your own unrivalled institutions in this field. One of the aspects of your system which has been most applauded is the technique of the case study, in which the students consider some specific situation in the affairs of a real or hypothetical company. I think the main merit of such a technique is that large generalizations are somewhat difficult to digest. By getting down to the particular we avoid compendious and rather meaningless terms, which serve to confuse rather than to enlighten us.

I do not see why the case study technique should not be just as relevant to political or economic situations. I would like, therefore, to talk to you today about 'A Case Study in the Special Relationship'. Most people would, I think, agree that in some respects the ties between the United States and Britain are of a distinctive character. At that point, however, agreement ends. Some sceptics believe that talk of a special relationship is at best irrelevant and at worst actually damaging; that the existence of these unusual ties is something of a distorting mirror, preventing us from seeing Anglo–American affairs as they really are. Others believe that the special relationship is the heart and core of all other alliances in which the two nations are involved.

What I want to do is to examine one part of this relationship as a kind of case study. Northern Ireland has an area comparable with Connecticut, and a population of around a million and a half. Within the British system of Government, it enjoys a rather special place, since it is the only part of the United Kingdom which has an essentially federal relationship with the central government. To explain how this came about, it is necessary to outline a certain amount of our history. It might be said that Northern Ireland, or Ulster as it is often called, is the creation of that process of pioneering and resettlement of population which also gave birth to the American colonies. The colonization of Ulster by English and particularly by Scottish settlers in the seventeenth century created there a new breed of people, distinctive in economic and social patterns from the bulk of the Irish population. When, therefore, the Irish nationalist movement sought and eventually won separation from the United Kingdom, we in Northern Ireland refused to break the ties of three centuries and continued our union with Great Britain. In 1920 a Government and Parliament were established in Belfast, with responsibility for most of our domestic affairs, but we continue to send members also to Parliament in London, and we do not exercise any powers in such fields as defence, foreign policy, or major taxation.

I am speaking, therefore, of an area which is distinctly British, but which also has its own special history, traditions and institutions. Let us examine Ulster as a case history in the special relationship.

First, there are the unusual and significant historic ties with the United States. The Scottish settlers in seventeenth-century Ulster were an upright breed of determined individualists. Theirs was an authoritarian century, and many of them had sought a new life in Northern Ireland to escape from the bonds of political, social and religious conformity. By the early eighteenth century it was evident to many of them that the full and free exercise of liberty which they sought would demand a still more drastic migration. And so, in the second decade of the eighteenth century, there began the emigration to America of that remarkable group of people known as the Scotch-Irish. Their main original settlements were in Pennsylvania. From there, they fanned out west and south, into Tennessee, Virginia and the Carolinas. Over a period of some sixty years at least 200,000 and probably a great many more sailed from the North of Ireland into American ports, so that by the time of the Declaration of Independence, not less than one in ten of the population of the colonies was of Scotch-Irish stock. Numerically, they were second only to the English settlers.

What kind of people were they? They were amongst the first of the early pioneers, ranging far beyond the limits of already settled land, clearing the virgin forest and planting their farms. In the war of Independence they were solidly behind the American cause, and in the years which followed they played a quite exceptional part in building this nation. We are naturally proud that the only Presidents who were first-generation Americans were also the sons of Ulster emigrants. Presidents Arthur, Buchanan, Cleveland, Grant, Harrison, Andrew Jackson, Andrew Johnson, McKinley, Polk and Woodrow Wilson were all of Scotch-Irish stock. In some cases the family homesteads in Northern Ireland are still standing today, and we are taking steps to see that they are properly preserved. The Scotch-Irish gave to America many more famous sons: Sam Houston of Texas, Davy Crockett the frontiersman, Stonewall Jackson, Andrew Mellon, Stephen Foster, Robert McCormick (inventor of the reaper) and 'Steamboat' Fulton. I might add that every one of these names can be found throughout the length and breadth of Northern Ireland today.

Here, then, is one thread of the 'special relationship'. In a sense it means more to us in Northern Ireland than it often does here, because although the role of the Scotch-Irish is well known by most Americans, far fewer are clear as to their origin. But they were, in fact, Ulstermen, and those of us who still live in Ulster have a deep sense of pride in the achievements of our sons in this great nation.

The second thread of the 'special relationship' is political and strategic. The military tradition of our small country is a remarkable one. In World War II there were five great Ulster soldiers, each of whom was to rise to Field Marshal—the highest rank in the British Army. They were Alexander and Montgomery, Alanbrooke, Auchinleck and Dill. Dill lies buried at Arlington National Cemetery. His part in forging the Anglo–American alliance was incalculable. But Ulster's strategic importance did not depend solely upon its ability to mass-produce Field Marshals. Northern Ireland was an essential staging-ground for the invasion of Europe. The first American troops to be sent to the European theatre of war arrived in Belfast, and altogether 300,000 were marshalled and trained in our midst. The ability to use Ulster in this way has been described by General Eisenhower himself as a vital factor in winning the war in Europe. With the Irish Republic maintaining its neutrality to the south of us, our airfields were of vital importance in protecting the eastern segment of the Atlantic sea lanes. Nor is this a thing of the past. Today, as a part of the United Kingdom, we are playing a vital role in NATO. Key installations and bases of the alliance are located within our territory, and in a situation where the Russian fleet is very heavily oriented towards submarines, I need not emphasize the strategic importance of our westerly position. I can assure you that Northern Ireland is one of the places—and, thank goodness, there are still many of them—where the presence of an American serviceman in uniform gives nothing but pleasure, and a sense of confidence in the strength and durability of our common traditions.

These historical and strategic ties give added significance to the third thread of the 'special relationship'—our business and commercial associations. As you know, Britain enjoyed over a very long period a great advantage over all other European countries as a location for American manufacturing industry. Indeed, until quite recently, there was as much direct investment in the United Kingdom as in all the other countries of Western Europe together. At the end of World War II, however, there was not a single American company with a plant in Northern Ireland. Within less than twenty years that situation has been completely transformed. Today, some of the most illustrious names in American industry are represented in Northern Ireland: Du Pont, I.T. & T., Ford, International Distillers and Chemical, Chemstrand, Hughes Tool and many others.

Because the American business movement in Europe has coincided with Ulster's drive for diversification, we have been able to watch the growth of a very substantial American business community in Northern Ireland. And it is at this point that the other two aspects of the 'special relationship' strengthen the third. Because of our political and strategic unity, American investment in Northern Ireland is completely safe from the perils of hostile nationalism which may beset it elsewhere. Because of our ancient historic ties, Americans feel at home in Northern Ireland and are accepted with enthusiasm into the local community.

I hope I have shown you that the 'special relationship' is more than a myth. It was born out of our common history, nurtured in our common experience, and thrives upon our common interests. It is a complex and many-sided relationship, but who can deny that in this century it has been a powerful force for good in the world?

(*The Bullock Forum, New York, 20th March 1964*)

O'Neill has seen in the story of the Scotch-Irish a source of inspiration and encouragement to generations of young Ulster men and women in the future.

The tale of the Scotch-Irish is no story of inherited riches or of easy success. It tells rather of a race of people whose later achievements were rooted in an early struggle for survival. The transition in one or two generations from the whitewashed cottage to the White House may seem almost a cliché—but it takes character to bridge that immense gulf, and it is upon their reserves of character that our two nations must chiefly depend. 'Automation' is a magic word; but no programmer, however mathematically sophisticated, can punch endurance on to a card or feed courage into a computer.

Some people may feel that all our efforts today should be concentrated upon the economic and technical challenges of the future. But if we lose pride in our past, if we fail to know our own forbears and cut the roots from which we have grown, our material rewards will turn to dust and ashes in our mouths.

I want the growing generation of children in the schools of

Ulster to be able to see and learn and understand that other generations, far less favoured than theirs, overcame all obstacles and sent their sons and grandsons to the highest elective office the world can offer. Even in an age of rocketry, there are more ways than one of reaching for the stars.

(*Opening of a Scotch-Irish Symposium, Belfast,*
24th September 1965)

Ulster people have also taken a considerable pride in the fact that it was in Northern Ireland that American troops first gathered for the ultimate invasion of Europe in World War II. The officially recorded first man ashore, on 25th January 1942, was Private First Class Milburn Henke. Twenty-five years later to the day, Mr. Henke returned to Belfast and was the guest of honour at a luncheon given by the Government. O'Neill used the occasion to refer to the close wartime relationship.

The occasion which we commemorate is a proud part of our history. We will always remember that Ulster represented the European pier of that trans-Atlantic bridge across which, in 1942, the might of America began to flow with increasing and ultimately irresistible force. By the end of the war, over 300,000 American troops were to be stationed here. In the winter of 1943/4 more than 120,000 were in Northern Ireland at the same time, representing about 1 in 10 of the whole civil population. And in addition to the use of Ulster as a training ground for troops, vital naval and air bases were set up to control the eastern approaches of the Atlantic. In November 1942, Mrs. Roosevelt visited the troops in Ulster, and in May 1944, the Supreme Commander, General Eisenhower, viewed the vast concourse of ships assembling in Belfast Lough prior to D-Day.

In November 1965, I had the great pleasure of meeting General Eisenhower in Atlanta in his capacity as President of the E.S.U. of the U.S. A few days ago I sent him this message:

'On 26th January we remember with pride and gratitude the 25th Anniversary of the arrival in Belfast of the first American troops to enter the European theatre of operations in World War II. As you said in Belfast at the end of the war: "From here started the long hard march to Allied victory." On this historic occasion we send you greetings as the architect of that victory, as a statesman of that great nation in which so many of our stock have flourished, and as a Freeman of our capital city. May the links made in peace and forged in war never weaken.'

I have today received the following reply:

'It is a privilege to send greetings to you as Belfast marks the 25th Anniversary of the first arrival in your State of American troops in World War II. I want to assure you and the gallant people you lead of the appreciation of every American who was privileged to enjoy the hospitality of Northern Ireland during that conflict. All of us remember that experience with gratitude and affection. With best wishes and high esteem.

(Signed)   DWIGHT D. EISENHOWER'

We were proud to stand beside our American allies in World War II; we are equally proud to stand again with them today in NATO. The history which records at least ten Presidents of Ulster stock; the commercial ties which are represented by so many American industries in our Province—these play a part in our links with the United States. But above all we recognize in her a great English-speaking nation, dedicated as we are to freedom under the law. From Magna Carta to the Gettysburg Address we discern a single tradition, and I hope a common destiny. No one knows how soon a tunnel may cross the Channel, but that symbolic trans-Atlantic bridge which brought our guest of honour to Ulster in 1942 shows no sign of weakening. May it continue to stand fast!

(Belfast, 26th January 1967)

CHAPTER 9

The Commonwealth and Europe

Although O'Neill has concentrated particularly upon Ulster–American ties, he has not neglected either the Commonwealth or Europe. His term of office has encompassed visits to Canada, and to a number of European countries including France and Germany.

The Prime Minister gave his views on Ulster's links with the Commonwealth at a dinner for the Commonwealth Press Union in 1964.

Lately it has become rather fashionable in some quarters to express a certain scepticism about the Commonwealth. A questioning spirit in examining established institutions is no bad thing, but I wonder whether those who are so eager to criticize the Commonwealth today can claim first-hand knowledge of its operations.

When you think of it, it is rather remarkable that the Government of this small country should have had so many Commonwealth contacts. I do not see how they would have been possible outside the Commonwealth setting. Since we do not conduct our own foreign affairs, in normal circumstances we could expect to have contacts almost entirely with our fellow citizens of Britain and our immediate neighbours on the Continent. There would be no setting in which we would meet the nations of Africa and America, Asia and Australasia. Yet it seems to me vital that this kind of meeting should take place. There is no place in the twentieth century for human tortoises who pull their heads back into their shells and refuse to see the community outside. The wind which rises in a distant continent today blows around the world tomorrow. In maintaining the peace, in expanding trade and investment, in conquering disease and hunger we need each other.

To me, the role of the Commonwealth as a forum in which the Continents may meet face to face informally is of supreme significance. In other settings, the nations meet more formally around the conference table. But, if friendship is the aim and understanding the goal, surely it is better to receive a man as a guest than as a delegate. Those who criticize the Commonwealth for its absence of formal machinery, who deplore its lack of unanimity and attack its conflicts of view, are surely missing its main point. In a world divided between competing alliances, its fundamental strength is that it is not an alliance. In an age which demands too much conformity, its very diversity is a reminder that men and nations may seek similar ends by very different means. Just as we hope, in our separate nations, to find ways in which the maximum freedom for the individual may be combined with the maximum of benefit to society, so within the Commonwealth our separate nations seek their own fulfilment in the wider international society.

I think you will find, if you study Northern Ireland and its way of life, that there is here a genuine and growing awareness of the interdependence of nations. This is a healthy spirit in an area such as ours, which earns its living by selling its goods all over the world. But our international links are not confined to enlightened self-interest in trade and commerce. Take, for example, the field of university education. Here, as elsewhere in Britain, there is a considerable and increasing pressure on university places. It would have been an easy matter to decide that our own students must have first preference, and that only if there was a surplus could outsiders be accommodated. But in fact our University has always accepted, and continues to accept, large numbers of overseas students, especially from Commonwealth countries. There are two reasons why this is a highly desirable practice. First, a university of all places cannot afford to be a closed society. The only frontiers by which it can be confined are the frontiers of knowledge itself. And secondly, it is a moral duty for the well-developed, richly endowed nations to assist the developing countries in an enlightened way.

Such an attitude is not mere sentimentality. Of course it is true that we have some stubborn local problems—as who does not?—and that these make heavy demands upon our resources of men and money. But we must get our priorities right. Local plans for progress will be of little avail if the world as a whole falls into anarchy.

We in Northern Ireland are very proud to be British. This Parliament Building in which we sit this evening would not exist but for our determination to continue to play our part in the United Kingdom. There are many reasons why we value that connection—some historical, some economic, some emotional. Not least amongst them is our feeling that only through Britain and the British Commonwealth can we look outwards rather than inwards, and associate ourselves with the great changes which are taking place in the world.

(*Belfast, 13th May 1964*)

One of the most moving occasions of O'Neill's premiership was the commemoration in 1966, on the battlefields of the First World War, of the fiftieth anniversary of the Battle of the Somme. In two speeches on 1st July, the anniversary itself, the Prime Minister paid his tribute to those who had fallen.

It is a tremendous honour and privilege for the Government of Northern Ireland to welcome today as its guests so many distinguished Frenchmen. In the ordinary course of events one would have some inhibitions about entertaining such a company in their own country. But here, at this place and above all at this time, we meet not as host and guest, not as citizen and foreigner, not as French and British, but as firm friends, ancient allies, tried and true comrades. Remembering as we do today the sacrifices which the best of our manhood have twice made side by side, there can be no barriers between us. Any differences of language, of tradition, of political attitude sink into insignificance when we recall what our two countries have suffered, and what they have achieved.

I welcome, too, the distinguished Ambassadors of the United Kingdom, Australia, Canada, the Irish Republic, New Zealand and South Africa, the Minister of Defence for the Army, and our other guests.

The ceremony which we have just witnessed, in its simple dignity, will remain long in the memories of all those who have seen it. Above all, it must have prompted poignant recollections in those veterans of the Battle of the Somme who have made the journey from Northern Ireland to be present. On this day fifty years ago the 36th (Ulster) Division went into battle in the Thiepval area. Their losses were terrible, but they won imperishable fame by their feats of courage. It is fitting that the Colonels of all the Northern Ireland Regiments should be with us on this occasion.

Of course, not all the veterans have been able to travel to France. Happily, the ceremony which we witnessed this morning will be repeated in Belfast on Monday, in the presence of Her Majesty The Queen and His Royal Highness the Duke of Edinburgh. Our French allies will be fittingly represented by a contingent of the French Navy.

This is not an occasion for lengthy speeches. The simple

words of the Service of Commemoration at the Ulster Tower represented a fitting tribute to the brave men whom we honour today. The freedom which we now enjoy is founded upon their sacrifice. Twice in this century Europe, which has given the world so much, has trembled upon the verge of irretrievable calamity. Now we have the third, and perhaps the last opportunity to work wisely together for common aims, so that all the courage and endurance of which man is capable may be applied to more constructive ends. Surely the magnificent but sad monuments which surround us here tell us mutely but eloquently where our duty lies.

(Amiens, 1st July 1966)

We are greatly honoured, M. le Prefet, by your invitation to dine with you at the Prefecture of the Somme. In our own capital city of Belfast, which I hope you may visit one day, we have a Picardy Avenue, a Somme Drive and a Thiepval Avenue. These are names which are part of our history as well as yours. Our veterans who have returned today to those fields in which they fought so bravely half a century ago are themselves survivors of those who survived. Fifty years is a long time, but for them these recollections can never be dimmed. I myself bear as my middle name that of another French battlefield, the Marne, as my mother was so thrilled with the results of the battle, which coincided with my christening.

We in Northern Ireland are extremely proud of our military traditions. From our small country, with a population of less than one and a half million today, have sprung many of the outstanding soldiers of the British Army. In recent times we can count Alexander, Montgomery, Alanbrooke, Dill, Templer—all Field Marshals and all of our stock. At a time such as this, however, we recall not only the great captains of war, but the anonymous thousands who fought and died not only here, but in every place where men have made their stand for freedom. History will record their collective deeds, even if it is silent as to their individual names.

In particular it is fitting to recall that on this day fifty years ago no fewer than four soldiers of the 36th (Ulster) Division performed deeds of valour on the battlefield which earned them the highest decoration for gallantry, the Victoria Cross. Three of the four gave their lives in the process, and on behalf of the people of Ulster I would wish to recall today the names of Captain Eric Bell, Lieutenant Geoffrey Cather, Private William McFadzean and Private Robert Quigg. They were amongst the bravest of the brave.

Ceremonies such as we have witnessed today cannot but make a profound impression upon those who were present. If all the courage, the endurance, the self-sacrifice, the idealism to which proper tribute has been paid could in future be harnessed to serve some wholly constructive cause, there could be few limits set to the potential progress of Europe. Over these battlefields, fifty years ago, fought the sons of three great European nations, each with its distinctive genius and its special gifts. We must never again dissipate our vital energies in such a struggle. If only Europe can remain true to itself, and become a fixed point of liberty in a changing world, the golden age of the European ideal may yet lie ahead of us. I speak this evening as Prime Minister of a small community—the farthest Atlantic bastion of the United Kingdom—and I say that those who ask of us what is our relationship to Europe will find a clear answer on the fields of the Somme.

(Amiens, 1st July 1966)

Many Canadian soldiers also fought on the Somme, as O'Neill was to recall in Toronto.

The saddest day of Ulster's history was 1st July 1916, when the Ulster Division went over the top at the Battle of the

Somme, and in heroic action suffered terrible losses. Their comrades from Canada and Newfoundland shed their blood over these same costly acres of ground. But was that not a proud day as well as a sad one? It showed that there were men in our own green island, and here across the broad Atlantic, who recognized a call to something greater than a purely local cause. To the farmer in the furrows of County Antrim or in the fertile fields of Canada, the quarrels of the European powers must have seemed at times a very remote thing. Yet they sensed that freedom around the world is indivisible and worth fighting for. They knew that the closest and most cherished things—family, friends, the small area one recognizes as home—can in the last resort only be protected by a willingness to serve wider causes and greater alliances.

(*Empire Club of Canada, Toronto, 19th October 1967*)

And on a visit to Germany in 1967, the Prime Minister spoke once more of the lesson of two world wars.

I know from personal experience what war can mean. My father fell in the First World War and my two brothers in the Second. Many of you who listen will have had similar experiences. I believe those experiences unite us in a conviction that such a thing must not happen again; that our strength must be used collectively to preserve the peace.

This is a time of great change and development in Europe. Fateful decisions have to be taken, which may determine the political and economic structure of our Continent for generations. Please note that I say *our* Continent. I speak for Northern Ireland, the most westerly Atlantic bastion of the United Kingdom, and I tell you tonight that we are Europeans with a European destiny.

It is not for me to say how that destiny is to be fulfilled. As Prime Minister of a 'Land' Government within the United

Kingdom, questions of national foreign policy are not my concern. I speak tonight only as a friend speaking to friends. My hope is that whatever the destiny of Europe, and of Britain in Europe may be, it will not have an exclusive or selfish basis. When a great force in the world pursues such a course, the world as a whole suffers for it. Is not the menacing danger of China due to the fact that it is a closed society? Should we not welcome a growing flexibility, however cautious, in Eastern Europe? Would the history of our times not have been very different if America had renounced isolationism earlier—or for that matter, continued it to this day?

A great force in the world must be outward-looking, generous, sympathetic. And Europe, however it is organized, must be such a force. Its aims must be positive, not negative or defensive. It must recognize its overwhelming obligations to the world of poverty at its gates.

(*Bonn, 2nd April 1967*)

CHAPTER 10

A View of the Future

O'Neill has spoken many times to young people of the wider prospects for their future. These two speeches exemplify the Prime Minister's thinking on these occasions.

I was greatly impressed to hear tonight that you have built your own school computer. Now a computer, as you know very well, is a very remarkable piece of equipment indeed—able to do in a split second calculations which would take even your best mathematics masters many hours. The world we live in depends a great deal on technical inventions of that kind. We have a Government computer centre of our own at Stormont, which works out all kinds of things which in the old days would have needed whole batteries of clerks.

Some people, when they see the development of these wonderful machines, become worried about the future of human beings. They ask if 'automation'—which means the process of replacing the human factor in many situations by a mechanical or electronic factor—will not mean fewer and fewer jobs. You have probably seen those science fiction films in which the robot suddenly develops a will of its own and gets out of control. A good many people wonder whether we are not—in a less dramatic way—creating a monster which will wreck our lives.

But, you know, thinking of this kind is nothing new. When

the old cottage industries of Britain were first replaced by machines gathered together in factories, a group of people called Luddites went around smashing the new machines. It seemed to them that when one machine could do the work of several men, the result must be fewer jobs and a harder life for the working people of Britain. Yet, looking back on it today, we can see that it was this Industrial Revolution which made Britain, by the second half of the nineteenth century, the richest and most powerful nation in the world. And it is still the case that the wealthy nations are not those in which vast populations perform prodigies of manual labour, but rather those in which science and technology are best developed. It is no accident that Japan, by far the most prosperous nation in Asia, is also that in which automation is by far the most advanced.

No country in the world can prosper if its people try to be twentieth-century Luddites. What we have to do is not to stand in the way of change, but to deal with some of its more harsh effects. In the long run, for instance, it is inevitable that other fuels should take the place of some of the coal we use. Having unlocked the secrets of nuclear power and tapped the resources of the North Sea, we cannot fail to exploit them.

These changes have come to Ulster too. Your fathers and grandfathers will remember the time when man and horse together worked the land. Today the fruits of the land are abundant beyond the dreams of thirty or forty years ago, but with mechanization, and particularly the tractor, far fewer men are needed to work that same land. That is why not every son of a farmer can today hope to follow his father's way of life, and why we want to create *new* openings for employment in *new* industries. We must obtain the biggest stake we can in expanding industries, the industries of tomorrow. And this we are doing—for instance a sixth of all the man-made fibres produced in Britain are made here in Northern Ireland.

From what I have said perhaps you may begin to think that there *is* a real danger of a world in which the machine will be king. If so, let me redress the balance. Countries achieve success not because they have clever machines, but because they have clever people who know how to invent and use them. Sir Frank Whittle is more important than the jet engine, Sir Alexander Fleming more useful than penicillin—because these were not machines but great human beings, with the capacity to go on to other fields and other tasks.

When people say to me, as they sometimes do, that Ulster is a very small place, I say that no place is small which can produce—as we have done so often—men who can earn the right to carry a British Field Marshal's baton or to sit in the White House as President of the United States.

Computers may be very rapid and very accurate, but it is human beings who ask the questions. And this is what education is about: teaching you to ask questions. Of course you need information too. But an educated person is not just a great big bag of facts. What is the good of knowing the distance from earth of every planet if you never lift your eyes to the stars?

Education is not something, either, which comes only in schools or universities. It comes from life itself. When I first became a junior Minister in the Government of Northern Ireland, I worked for a very great man, Billy Grant, who was then Minister of Health. His university had been the Queen's Island shipyard. He may not have had an extensive knowledge of Greek verbs, but he was rich in knowledge and experience of life. He could cut through some apparently complex issue because he knew how to ask simple direct common-sense questions.

This is what our country needs today more than ever— people who question things. If you leave this school determined to examine things for yourself, and not just to accept other people's prejudices, then you will be a truly valuable member of society. 'Loyalty to what is true' might not be a bad motto in this life. For the computer and all the scientific wonders of this age do not limit the usefulness of the human intelligence; rather do they extend its reach. The spirit which has taken man to the top of the highest mountain and the depths of the sea, and which has now brought the moon within his grasp—this spirit of daring and inquiry is what we need to face other challenges nearer to home.

(*Mountcollyer Secondary School, Belfast,
2nd February 1968*)

As we watch the television news or read a paper, the impression is often depressing. War, riot, famine, disturbance—these things seem to monopolize the screen. It is hardly surprising that young people growing up in this environment are often troubled about their future, and the future of the world.

Certainly this is a troubled time. Science has with one hand increased our power to kill each other, and with the other greatly increased the expectation of life in many parts of the world. A great question mark hangs over our ability to solve these problems of war and over-population.

But if these particular problems have entered a new dimension, this does not mean that the challenge and danger of living is a new thing. That is why I hope those of you who study history do not look upon it as just a dull list of kings and battles. What it can teach you, amongst other things, is that *every* age in man's life on earth has been an age of danger and challenge.

The Victorian Age may seem a long era of peace and prosperity for Britain when we look back upon it now. But apart from the unutterable squalor and misery in which a large part of the population lived, the people of that day always felt themselves to be on the verge of great dangers. It was by no means an uninterrupted time of peace.

N*   195

A VIEW OF THE FUTURE

Take, for example, the world as it looked 100 years ago, in 1868. The new menace on the horizon was the growing power of Germany, soon to be locked in battle with France. Here in Ireland there was growing agitation and discontent. And in distant America the United States was starting to bind up the wounds of an awful civil war.

Go back a century at a time—to 1768, 1668 and beyond, and you will find a similar story. Peace on earth, and in every part of it, has always been a dream, never a complete reality.

I am not saying this to be depressing, but to show that there is nothing unique about the element of strain and danger in human life today. It has always been present. Men have constantly foretold the doom of this nation or that. But mankind survives, and in a patient fashion rebuilds upon the foundations of what is destroyed.

Germany, twice utterly defeated and the second time completely devastated in a period of fifty years, has risen again to new levels of prosperity. France's proud and self-confident attitude today buries the memory of her humiliation of a quarter of a century ago.

Medieval Britain lost her French possessions but went on to defeat the Armada; eighteenth-century Britain lost the American colonies, but Wellington beat Napoleon at Waterloo; twentieth-century Britain has shed her Empire, and again voices say that we are finished. But a nation is never finished as long as it has people of brains and energy and imagination.

A nation grows like an old, well-established tree. The gales batter it, and sometimes a branch may fall, but it has its roots deep in the earth. When the weather changes to the frosts of winter it is laid bare; but always the spring comes and there is a new flowering.

So my advice to the young people growing to maturity in this generation is: by all means feel concerned about the state of your country and the world, but never despair of it. In

196

every age men have shown their greatest qualities when challenged and tested.

Today, as always, it is the people who matter and human
qualities which count. Every time I visit a school, I find it
exciting to think that someone in the audience may have the
potential to achieve great things. I wish I could meet you all
again twenty-five years from now to see what you have done
with your talents, but that is hardly likely to happen!

What is certain is that here at home in Ulster there are more
openings than ever before for people of very different qualifi-
cations. Fifty years ago the Ulster population was fairly stereo-
typed: the farmer or farm labourer; the mill girl; the shipyard
worker.

But now the country cries out for talent of all kinds: for
research experts to staff its universities; engineers to build its
roads and bridges; technologists to operate its new, science-
based industries; yes, and poets and playwrights, actors and
sculptors too.

We want the new Ulster to be not just a construction of
bricks and mortar but a work of the spirit and the imagination,
a good place as well as a prosperous one.

I began with the dangers of the age; let me end with its
excitement. What will you see as you live out these remaining
years of the twentieth century? Man on the moon, certainly;
the Atlantic reduced to a mere stream by the speed of travel;
the cure, I hope, for many of the diseases which ravage us
today; perhaps a new insight into the nature of life itself. You
can look forward to enjoying great books as yet unwritten,
hearing great music as yet uncomposed.

So, in spite of all the perils which exist, my advice to you is
to face life not with concern, but with eagerness. There are
great problems, certainly, but I look to your generation to find
many of the answers.

(*Magherafelt Secondary School, 21st March 1968*)

Resignation

The indeterminate result of the General Election left O'Neill in an unenviable position, since he had to face both divisions in the governing party and continuing unrest in the streets. Although he was able to carry a majority of the Parliamentary Party with him, further votes of confidence in external party bodies revealed the existence of strong and determined minorities in opposition to his leadership. The situation came to a head amidst acts of terrorist violence against vital water and electricity supply installations, and further serious street clashes in Londonderry. Units of the Army had to be called in to guard key installations, and growing uneasiness about the deteriorating Ulster situation was expressed at Westminster.

O'Neill decided that a further effort must be made to take the heat out of the situation, and on 23rd April 1969 he announced to the House of Commons that the Government had accepted the principle of 'one man, one vote' (the principal demand of the 'civil rights' movement), to be applied at the next local government elections, and that he would either implement this key reform or resign.

Although the Unionist Parliamentary Party accepted this change of policy by a narrow majority, O'Neill's position was gravely weakened by the resignation of one of his leading Ministers, Major James Chichester-Clark, who accepted the principle of uni-

198

*versal adult suffrage but felt the timing of this decision to be
inopportune. The Prime Minister was committed to place the new
policy before the Standing Committee of the Ulster Unionist
Council and the full Council itself, and it began to appear increasingly doubtful that he could surmount both these political
hurdles without a further loss of parliamentary support. Nevertheless it came as a great surprise when, on 28th April, Captain
O'Neill announced that he had resigned the leadership of the
Unionist Party, and, once a successor had been elected, would
step down as Prime Minister. 'A new leader', he observed, 'committed on his record to progressive principles but unhampered by
personal animosities, may have a better chance of carrying on the
work which I have begun.'*

*The following evening, O'Neill took his farewell of the people
of Northern Ireland in a television broadcast.*

I am speaking to you tonight as your Prime Minister for the
last time. As you know, I have resigned the leadership of the
Unionist Party and, as soon as my successor is elected, I will
be giving up the Premiership.

To those of you who have so loyally supported me, who in
times of trouble have sent me countless letters, telegrams and
other messages, I want to say this: Do not be dismayed. What
you and I were trying to do together was right. Morally right,
politically right, right for our country and all who seek to live
in peace within it.

Justice, equality, generosity—these are enduring standards,
and it is far more important to proclaim them than to sit on the
fence, wondering which way to jump. But any leader who
wants to follow a course of change can only go so far. For
change is an uncomfortable thing to many people, and inevitably one builds up a barrier of resentment and resistance
which can make further progress impossible.

In my judgment—and in that of my good friends whom I

have consulted—I have reached that moment. What is now impossible for me may be—I do not know—easier for someone else. But I have no regrets for six years in which I have tried to break the chains of ancient hatreds. I have been unable to realize during my period of office all that I had sought to achieve. Whether, now, it can be achieved in my lifetime I do not know. But one day these things will be and must be achieved.

All arguments about the form and personnel of Government are irrelevant when matched against one simple truth. Here we are, in this small country of ours, Protestant and Catholic, committed by history to live side by side. No solution based on the ascendancy of any section of our community can hope to endure. Either we live in peace, or we have no life worth living.

For too long we have been torn and divided. Ours is called a Christian country. We could have enriched our politics with our Christianity; but far too often we have debased our Christianity with our politics. We seem to have forgotten that love of neighbour stands beside love of God as a fundamental principle of our religion. I was moved, as many of you must have been, to see the leading clergy of Derry, Protestant and Roman Catholic, side by side in the streets of that troubled city. This simple act of Christian friendship was a shining example of what would have been possible, but for the machinations of wicked men who have preached and practised hatred in the name of God.

A few short weeks ago you, the people of Ulster, went to the polls. I called that Election to afford you the chance to break out of the mould of sectarian politics once and for all. In many places, old fears, old prejudices and old loyalties were too strong. Yet I am not amongst those who say that the Election served no useful purpose. For it did allow me, with my loyal colleagues, to proclaim a new Declaration of Principles which now binds every Unionist returned to Parliament. It speaks in clear terms of justice and equality; it commits the Party, in honour and in conscience, not merely to do nothing to enlarge the divisions of our community, but to work positively to end them. You will be watching, as I will be, to see to it that these pledges are honoured.

There *is* no other course. Democratic government must rest upon the consent not just of those who elect the governing party, but of the people as a whole. And I remind you once again, as I have done so often before, that Ulster is not a rich, powerful, independent state, but a part of the United Kingdom committed to United Kingdom standards and subject in the last resort to United Kingdom authority. We *must* go forward; for British public and parliamentary opinion would not tolerate our going back.

And now the time has come for me to say farewell. My wish for you—for the Province we all love so much—is for peace. We must pray for peace and we must also work for it: the politician in Parliament, the clergy in the churches, the working people in our farms and factories. Look about you at the present state of our country, and try to answer the question: 'Is this *really* the kind of Ulster that you want?' I asked you that question once before; and now, as then, it is only you who can answer.

On 1st May the Unionist Parliamentary Party met to choose its new leader. By the narrowest of margins, 17 votes to 16, Major James Chichester-Clark was chosen in preference to Mr. Brian Faulkner. Later that day, Captain Terence O'Neill travelled to Government House to submit his resignation to the Governor. The O'Neill years were over. Ulster clearly remained at the cross-roads. But to many the words and the deeds of his premiership represented the only way ahead.